TRACKS

TRACKS

Journeys in Time and Place

GENNI GUNN

Cover design by Doowah Design.
Photo of Genni Gunn by Tom Hawkins Photography.

Acknowledgements
Some of these stories have been previously published: "Tracks," *Numéro Cinq*; "Sundays," *Room of One's Own*, "Crostoli," *Italians-Canadians At Table* (Guernica Editions); "Tracks," *Slice Me Some Truth*, edited by Zoë Landale and Luanne Armstrong (Wolsak and Wynn).

Many thanks to Karen Haughian for insightful editing, to my agent Carolyn Swayze for continued support, and to my travel/soul mate, Frank for being there.

This book was printed on Ancient Forest Friendly paper.
Printed and bound in Canada by Hignell Book Printing Inc.

We acknowledge the support of the Canada Council for the Arts and the Manitoba Arts Council for our publishing program.

Library and Archives Canada Cataloguing in Publication

Gunn, Genni, author
     Tracks : journeys in time and place / Genni Gunn.

Issued in print and electronic formats.
ISBN 978-1-927426-32-6 (pbk.).—ISBN 978-1-927426-33-3 (epub)

1. Gunn, Genni – Travel. 2. Gunn, Genni – Family. 3. Authors, Canadian (English) – 20th century – Travel. 4. Voyages and travels. I. Title.

PS8563.U572Z85 2013   C818'.5403   C2013-905429-4
                                                                    C2013-905430-8

Signature Editions
P.O. Box 206, RPO Corydon, Winnipeg, Manitoba, R3M 3S7
www.signature-editions.com

CONTENTS

FOREWORD

... if every true love affair can feel like a journey
to a foreign country, where you can't quite speak the
language, and you don't know where you're going,
and you're pulled ever deeper into the inviting darkness,
every trip to a foreign country can be a love affair,
where you're left puzzling over who you are and
whom you've fallen in love with.

—Pico Iyer

When I think of travel, I don't think of destinations, I think of movement, of assuaging restlessness, of being rootless, as immigrants are, always reaching for that elusive imagined *home,* like trying to catch a mirage on a hot desert highway, the illusion shimmering and enticing.

For some, travel is a fearful thing, a possibility of being stranded outside one's comfort zone. Once, during a fiction workshop I was teaching, a student submitted a story in which the protagonist, given an opportunity to spend the summer in Paris working for his uncle, refuses to go. I was puzzled. Because within the story there was no evidence of emotional or psychological reasons for the protagonist's reluctance, I asked the student why a young man would not leap at the chance to go to France.

"What if he gets stuck in Paris?" he replied.

The student I spoke to lives in a Vancouver suburb and considers Vancouver a distant place, unfamiliar and dangerous. Yet, by placing himself outside his comfort zone, he would be forced to pay attention, to be more aware, because as Cesare Pavese says, travel keeps you "constantly off balance. Nothing is yours except the essential things — air, sleep, dreams, the sea, the sky — all things tending towards the eternal or what we imagine of it."

Travel for me is a comfortable state, a detachment from the trappings of a physical place. It's the motion I crave, the to-and-fro, taking flight and landing, going to cities or countries, towards new landscapes and emotional terrains, because when one travels, the unknown awaits to be discovered — about one's self, about others, about one's relationship to time and place.

When I was younger, for many years I travelled across Canada, a musician playing in a myriad of bands: one-nighters in capital cities, ten-week tours in the north and east and west and south. That was a different kind of travel, a journey into music and myself, my days spent alone, my nights on stage; the public performer and the private person, a clear distinction. But on those night drives while everyone slept, I was re-energized; as the roadsides vanished into dark, I felt as if I were alone in the universe, the steering wheel under my hands, the road snaking black into forever.

Sometimes, I travel to explore new landscapes, the sea, the sky, the natural world a perfect metaphor for memory, for (e)motions, for relationships, for all that is in endless motion and change. Nature is organic and as close to perfect in its properties as anything could be. In the intricate design of a leaf or a tree trunk is art and architecture, texture and colour; in any living thing is the constant metamorphosing, the visible stages of birth, life and death, evident within a moment, or a season, or a month or a year. All life, a three-stage play of beginning, middle and end. I leave home, I travel, I return.

And if I stay away long enough, on my return, home reappears slightly altered, discordant, a melody played in the wrong key. For a while, I feel unsettled — the city louder, greyer, the people strange. I long for solitude and open spaces, recreating myself elsewhere in memory, until slowly I settle into the busyness of my city life.

Sometimes, as I cross the bridge that connects downtown with North and West Vancouver, I pretend I'm in a foreign city, struck by how exquisite and exotic the city feels, with its port, its mountains of yellow sulphur and black coal, the harbour a palette of primary colours, of rusting hulls and huge container ships loading and unloading, coming and going, as if created from the whimsical brush of a painter. It's like seeing it for the first time. And I think that if this were a different city, an unknown place, I'd long to live here, where solemn skyscrapers — their glass faces mirroring a distant horizon — rise against the green and blue of mountains falling into the sea. But this pretending game is only that, a game. Always the restlessness returns, the instinct to fight stasis, the yearning for metamorphosis.

Sometimes I travel to enter a state of alienation — an anonymity that reflects my restlessness, my need for diverse landscapes, new experiences, not as flights to and from anything, nor as quests, but as journeys into the unexpected, through which even the ordinary becomes extraordinary, as if an opaque film has been removed from my eyes, rendering my vision more acute. In Sittwe, outside my window, a tree heavy with hanging fruit bats appears miraculous, as if it had borne the breathing creatures that cling to its branches until dark; scarlet lava flowing into the sea in a thunderhead of vapour in Hawaii is a sharp reminder of the earth's fearsome power. In the hills of Myanmar, I jump to safety when water buffalo approach, then realize they are afraid of me. Nothing is what it seems, my perceptions in continual flux. Motion is my aphrodisiac: the possibility of discovery versus the claustrophobia of continuity. The unknown, a constant attraction/distraction.

We travel, Pico Iyer says, "in part just to shake up our complacencies by seeing all the moral and political urgencies, the life-and-death dilemmas, that we seldom have to face at home." Travel makes us better citizens, more aware of the inequities present, of our own privileged existence.

In foreign countries, we place ourselves in the hands of strangers, and trust them. We enter villagers' houses and sleep on monastery floors; we listen to stories we'd never find in newspapers or web postings. We delight in the Buddhist chants of children at dawn, in the exotic flora; and, away from cities, where men and women labour in the fields morning till night, we are reminded of the enormous gap between their lifestyle and ours — a gap that seems insurmountable.

Because my sister was living in Myanmar, my travels there in the years before the election were not only an opportunity to reconnect with her, but also to visit a country closed to the outside world for decades, to glimpse the evolving political landscape and the effects of events that led up to the election of 2010. These were journeys into the foreign, into uncertainty, into mystery — the antithesis of our media-saturated, technological, reality-TV, public artifice. In Myanmar, my sister and I remembered our child selves, and recounted who we were, mixing and matching our memories, as if to rediscover each other.

When I was seven, and my sister Ileana was eight and a half, my aunt Ida took us by train to Naples and put us aboard an ocean liner bound for Halifax. As the departure time got closer, my aunt suddenly realized that we had no toys to play with on the long ten-day journey across the ocean. She bade us to wait quietly for a moment, while she rushed into a store nearby and bought coloured paper and scissors. On her return, she had barely time to give us the paper before we were herded up into the ship by a young woman who also was on her way to Canada. My aunt claims that Ileana and I were so delighted by our paper and scissors that we didn't even wave goodbye.

I don't think we were as cruel as my aunt describes, her heart broken by our disregard. For the first time in our lives, we were going to live with our parents in Canada — a name that became synonymous with family and home — although I don't think at the time we realized that this reunion was being effected because my father, who was thirty, had had a heart attack and my mother had joined him a few months earlier, in a panic, thinking he would die.

This was certainly not the first journey I had taken. Ever since I can remember, my sister and I have travelled to visit each other. We lived most of our childhood in Italy apart, Ileana in northern Italy in Udine with our grandparents, and I in southern Italy in Rutigliano with an aunt. However, several times each year, one of us would travel to visit the other, and we would spend a month or so together. My parents were in constant movement; they delighted me with their arrivals and, with their departures, left me in a permanent state of longing.

This longing has now transcended people and countries, and become a need that propels me forward to foreign lands, new experiences, in the search for connection. And I come close, in many ways, so often. But soon, the magnetic pull returns, this never-ending longing for home.

To Italy, I travel often, because Italy, for me, is a search: a return to the echoes of childhood — both familiar and foreign — given that my parents, sister and I never lived together in a house in Italy. A search, perhaps, for a mythical *home* — that ghost town I populate with the memories of those who knew me then, their version of me more palpable than my version of myself. Each return leads me to a slightly altered place, a *fata morgana* of hilltop towns and cliffs toppling into the sea, of experiences distorted and magnified, unlike the ones fixed inside the snow-globe of memory.

All/none of Italy is home. From year to year, it is an adjustment, a re-evaluation, both of myself and others. Udine, for example, is the home of my father, where I spent many childhood summers playing in its large garden (now Eden in memory). I return, to the same house, the same garden, a homecoming to family and childhood, although neither exist in the present, the people, long gone, or so altered, memory is all that remains, and this is a dangerous thing, because memory is like the earth — in constant formation, mutation —year to year: stone falls, ice melts into flash floods, heavy rain furrows the paths. And we, too, are mutable as sandstone, made of the compressed debris of our past, which is unstable and shifts and buckles and liquefies under pressure.

In travel, I search for the unstable ground, the fault lines, the deepest caves that echo my inner journey.

ESCAP(AD)ES

If we are always arriving and departing, it is also true that we are eternally anchored. One's destination is never a place but rather a new way of looking at things.

— Henry Miller

SUNDAYS

The spring I turned twelve, my father bought an 8mm movie camera and began to record our Sunday family outings with the diligence of a historian and the imagination of an artist. He labelled and dated each reel, yet what he filmed was a whimsical rendition of truths: a clearcut of stumps recast as a battlefield; an abandoned hornet's nest transformed into a condominium complex on the side of a cliff; or my mother sitting motionless in the woods disguised as a bear. Then there were skits, inventions for the camera, all against the backdrop of luxurious green forest, pebble beaches and the blue-black waters of the BC coast. Thus, our first four years in Canada are indelible illusions in 8-minute segments, which capture us in eternal vaga(bondage).

As soon as the snow melted and the roads became passable, no matter what the weather, my mother would pack sandwiches, drinks and fruit, and my father would urge us into the car toward an unknown destination. To amuse us, perhaps, Father invented the Sunday Picnic Tradition, one, he told us, that had been in his family for so many generations, no one knew exactly when it began, but might well go back to the beginning of time. And so, I imagined apes and cavemen and Adam and Eve packing raw fish and meat into fig leaves; I imagined entire families swinging through jungles and softly landing in green meadows beside translucent pools and shimmering waves; I imagined picnics and magnificent tigers sunning nearby. Perhaps our excursions were my father's way of making us a family — trapped as we were inside the car on the drive to and from our destinations.

When my father died, my mother sealed our Sundays into a large box in the storage sub-basement. And so, my first Canadian memories, like my father, remained undisturbed for two decades, until my mother moved.

And suddenly, here she is in Vancouver, our past bulging in boxes, and it's a resurrection — even my father's body disinterred and reburied here in warmer soil, because my father hated cold; every two or three years since his arrival in Canada, he had returned to Italy in summer, to olive trees and Adriatic sands.

TRACKS

Now we blow off the shroud of dust, peel back the tape and, in the middle of the move, set up the old projector. We sit on boxes, gather round and watch furtive moments flash by, like selected memories or lies. What I recall are not the visuals—the wooden movements, the fixed smiles, the antics created for the camera—but all that went before and after: my father's laughter, his insatiable curiosity and craving for new experiences; my mother's sensuality, her wild imagination. Our coming to Canada was the latest in a series of displacements that had us in constant movement.

The film begins with a panoramic view of Kitimat, 1962, originally a company town constructed around the Alcan Aluminum Smelter. Down the hill in Kildala, a shopping centre boasts six businesses—a Hudson's Bay Company, a pharmacy, a menswear store, a hairdresser, a jeweller (to provide engagement rings and wedding bands to each graduating class), and a Brides! store to supply the white gowns, often with empire waists and generous folds to conceal pregnancies. Further along the highway, near Kitimat River and away from the residential part of town, looms the Kitimat hotel, with its beer parlours strategically located halfway between the Alcan Smelter and the town—a stopover after work. Around the hotel are lumberyards, ironworks, mechanics' shops, snowplows and backhoes. In between the hotel and the town is a motel to house the transient young men who come to work at the smelter for the summers.

How we came to be here is a long and winding story that begins with my father working with the British Intelligence Corps during the war years, and ends with his relocation to a Commonwealth country. How strange Canada must have seemed to him. I was too young to ask questions, and he was probably not at liberty to answer them. So there we were in Kitimat. Remote and inaccessible to outside influences, it sealed the inside in, like the pots in the aluminum smelter—sputtering with molten metal—which now and then splashed onto the exposed skin between glove and sleeve, between collar and hair. And I think I can smell it now, skin burning, smell it strong as the stench of bigotry, of righteousness, those insidious scents, identity cards to a restricted club. And I, excluded (even years later when I left my Kitimat husband and escaped), ostracized by those people with whom I'd gone to school, as if they feared that my proximity would leave them sullied, contaminated. As if they might catch the dis-ease, might suddenly have to admit that lives don't always pan out well; that it's easy to make mistakes; that marriages and families and memories are like sand dollars found on beaches and brought home: fragile and beautiful.

There was no escape back then, not physical at least. To reach Kitimat from Vancouver by car, one had to travel up the old Fraser River Canyon road—a treacherous one-laner—760 kilometres to Prince George. Then left, for another 630 kilometres. The last stretch comprised over 150 kilometres of gravel road — mostly blasting chips — which punctured tires and shattered windshields. Kitimat, the final stop on the highway. There should have been a warning sign, DEAD END. Inaccessible. Perhaps our excursions were my father's way of transcending isolation.

In these illusions, the wilderness is elusive in the camera's eye. Outside the frame, the earth was verdant and swollen with creeks, rivers and lakes, a microcosm of Canada we explored on Sundays. We scoured the black gravel beaches along the Channel — a long arm of the sea, deep enough for the freighters which carried bauxite to the Alcan aluminum smelter. I always found it difficult to imagine that this black water, so like a large river whose opposite banks I could see, was really part of the ocean. The sea I had crossed years before was an endless horizon of blue rising to meet the blue of sky, of air. In Kitimat, the Channel was choppy and murky, surrounded by dense forest, crowned by the thick black smoke emanating from the smelter stacks.

And there we are, one Sunday, our picnic set on logs, in plain view of the smelter. My father sits on a boulder, a book on his lap, watching the tide come in. In the distance, my sister and I explore the charred remains of the old hospital, whose concrete foundations delineate wards and hallways. We had seen photographs of this hospital taken in the 1950s, before the town was built. My father had walked us through the ruins and mapped out his room. "The priest had come; your mother and I had said our goodbyes," he said with a Lazarus smile. "But I fooled them all." This was his first resurrection, five years before. Cardiac arrest. The heart imprisoned in a foreign country, but present in these clips — eternal resurrections at the flick of a switch.

Genni & Ileana at Hirsch Creek, Kitimat, BC

TRACKS

There we are, my sister and I scrambling among the debris, imagining ourselves doctors, deftly attending to war wounded, or staving off cholera. Not once did we think of ourselves as nurses. Our parents were equal partners. Both worked; both cooked and did housework; both had travelled extensively and not together; and both took responsibility for their actions, and expected the same of us. I don't recall religion or tradition ever offered as an excuse for anything. What I do recall are canvases leaning against easels throughout the house, and opera blaring from the speakers; my mother and father sitting side by side in a kitchen nook, painting together, sometimes not speaking for hours. My mother's paintings were landscapes in greens and blues then, while my father's were human forms with distorted features, in yellows and corals. Both existed in harmony while maintaining their individuality.

In music, while unison requires instruments to play the same note, it is the individual — the different — tones that make harmony. In our family no unison was possible. On those Sunday drives to the picnic sites, our car transformed into a mini concert hall for choral performances. Father was the baritone, Mother the tenor, my sister the soprano and I the alto. We never tired of singing the same repertoire, which was long enough to last several hours. We did renditions of Italian pop and folk songs, Fruilani mountain songs whose words only my father understood, and English folk ballads learned at school. Music was our common language, a melodic penetration into foreignness. No one ever spoke in our car. We sang our harmonies and stifled our quarrels. My sister and I were best friends and allies even then.

This next home movie was taken at Hirsch Creek, ten kilometres out of Kitimat. I recognize the massive trees towering like sentinels, ominous yet strangely comforting. The trail, chocolate brown, strewn with pine cones and needles. There was no underbrush; no sun could filter through the thick upper foliage. Here and there gnarled roots protruded from the ground in intricate sculptures, or intertwined to form dangerous traps. Scattered throughout were fallen trees — rotted and moss-covered. Some were entirely hollow, and I imagined they might be bear dens, and often approached them in delirious anticipation. In the forest I felt safe. Bears were part of the landscape, like rotting trees which could fall in a windstorm, or dangerous rapids with undertows. Respected, but never feared. The things I feared were abstract: separation, death.

Sometimes, my sister and I would try to wade into the creek to see how fast the current was, or how deep the water. But we never managed more than a couple of feet, because the water was frigid, spring or summer, so frigid that our feet were numbed almost immediately. My mother kept her flip-flops on and stepped gingerly on the rocks along the shore. Only my father would wade in slowly until the water reached his waist, then would

SUNDAYS

Genni and Ileana with dog Ricky, at Kitimat River, Kitimat, BC

submerge himself in one quick plunge, before coming out to dry in the sun. Then, he would tell us about the Adriatic Sea, re-forming our memories of aquamarine water, white beaches and golden sun absorbed into pink and coral roofs.

And in this reel, it must be summer because I can see the small pockets of warm water. The creek would swell on rainy days and flow swiftly over the entire bed. But after a few weeks of drought, the higher ground of the creek bed would dry and form pools which could neither be replenished nor escape. It was in these pools that my sister and I would wade and swim and play, imagining ourselves at Miramar, near Trieste. We had shovels and pails, but instead of sand, we collected rocks and twigs and squiggly worms. The latter we trapped in jars which we took home and left on the porch until one of our parents emptied them.

In late spring, these pools were filled with salmon — with females, pathetic and sluggish, awaiting death after spawning. I could never understand why we couldn't lift them out of the water where they swam, docile and lazy, and take them home for supper. Perhaps it was the death in them. For weeks, the creek banks emanated the stench of rotting fish. We walked, careful to avoid the carcasses on rocks. In this reel, the fish are squirming in my father's hands. It's an illusion. My father, who did not fish, discovered two massive salmon floating belly up and not yet decomposed. The home movie shows him in his bathing trunks holding a salmon in each hand, straining under the weight. For months, he showed the movie and told everyone he'd caught them that afternoon.

TRACKS

One year, I remember, on the first Sunday outing in spring when the snow had barely cleared, we found, at the entrance to the picnic area, a large wooden sign proclaiming HIRSCH CREEK, as if it were something new. Beside it, a peculiar sculpture made of five steel rods, four metres high and one metre wide. Randomly welded onto the front and back face were steel diamond shapes of about eight inches — a bizarre harlequin costume dredged up from memories of Italian feasts and town parades. My father filmed it at odd angles so that it became a jagged mountain top, a futuristic city in space, and a scaly prehistoric monster. My mother, sister and I immediately clambered onto it, grasping the tips of the diamonds, racing to the top. And there we are, halfway up, smiling at the camera, waving to my father. The film captured the sight, but not the sound, which I recall vividly. My sister was standing on my mother's foot, and my mother was shouting in pain, between gritted teeth and smiling, crimson lips.

And now, a splice, Kitimat River, thirty kilometres out of town. In colour. A year or two later. As if my father were tired of black and white; yearned, perhaps, for the diversity of colour. This river, a constant variation.

Genni, her father, Leo (right) and family friend at Hirsch Creek, Kitimat, BC

SUNDAYS

Once, it had cut a half-mile swath through the forest. Now, water flowed only in one portion of the bed — deep and swift, rippling across stones beneath the surface; so noisy that we had to shout to hear each other. The rest was an expanse of rounded stones on which my father manoeuvred the car, careful not to puncture the tires. From one visit to the next, the river could transform itself. Depending on rainfall, or fallen logs, it might start rushing in a new direction, split into two, and make islands in the middle. This was one of my favourite spots, because no matter how often we came, we could always find unexplored territory, the land in constant metamorphosis.

Look, there's my mother wearing her waterskier smile for the next illusion. She didn't know how to swim, yet she loved water. On this day, she asked my father to film her at the edge of the river. She faced him, and with her body mimicked the movements of a water-skier traversing waves at high speeds. Her arms were stretched taut in front of her, holding an imaginary line; her body swung gracefully side-to-side, distributing her weight on imaginary skis. My father was supposed to film her from mid-calves, so that the river behind her could create the full illusion. Which didn't happen, because he captured the entire scenario, now locked forever on film. "And there's your mother water-skiing on rocks," I hear him say then, now, in and around the film, all of us laughing and begging for replays.

This is what I remember most: laughter and music, our family, a gypsy troupe forging into unknown territory. Perhaps our excursions were my father's way of reinventing us Sunday to Sunday, country to country. Those massive riverbeds have become familiar landscapes in my dreams. Often, I find myself scrambling across the stones, anxious to reach, perhaps, a Sunday captured in the black and white celluloid of an old home movie.

OUROBOROS

I have no photos, no film, no videos of the journeys during my twenties and early thirties, when I travelled ten to eleven months a year, crisscrossing Canada as a rock musician, *on tour,* as the agents called it. The words *on tour* conjure tall, air-conditioned buses with smoked windows, Internet access and on-board toilets; hotel rooms with impeccable sheets and starched pillowcases; windows with a view of the sea, or the mountains, or whatever; audio-guide visits to museums, art galleries and famous/infamous dead people's homes. We were *on the road*, on hard grey asphalt from Vancouver to Newfoundland, though most often, our travels occurred in Western Canada: Vancouver, Kamloops, Kelowna, Vernon, Calgary, Red Deer, Edmonton, Grande Prairie, Fort St. John, Medicine Hat; some continued on to Swift Current, Saskatoon, Regina, Winnipeg; and others further still to Kapuskasing, North Bay, Toronto, Montreal, Fredericton, Saint John, Halifax, St. John's, Corner Book.

Those twelve years on the road — the trips back and forth across the country — have become one long journey in memory, city to city, bar to bar, 624 weeks of setting up on Sunday, playing Monday to Saturday, tearing down Saturday night, driving, driving, driving to the next gig. Set up. Play. Tear down. Drive. Same venues, same people, same same. After the first few road trips, the novelty evaporated, and people ceased to be individuals, towns ceased to have names, dates ceased to exist. I was aware only of Sundays (when we set up) and Saturday nights (when we tore down and drove all night, all day, sometimes all night again).

I was the night driver. It was the best time, night: the silence, and everyone asleep. The road streamed before me, boundless and mysterious, to the edge of the forests, the gullies, the deserts and lakes, the Canadian landscape as varied and ominous as our musician life was repetitive and predictable: each night, we played till 2:00 a.m., then wound down for a couple of hours, slept till noon the next day, rehearsed all afternoon, ate at the cheapest salad bar in town, showered, dressed, and were on stage by 9:00 p.m. There was no time to hike or sightsee, to swim, see movies, attend barbeques and birthday parties. We barely noticed the life transpiring outside bars and taverns, caught as we were in a whirl of beer-stained carpets, burly bouncers, skimpily dressed waitresses, and drunken patrons, coloured lights softening the edges of everything.

I had entered this parallel world in love with music, having sung and played piano since a child. I chose bass guitar as instrument because I adored its depth, and its essentiality — the backbone of the band, rather than a frill (which, at that time, is how women in bands were perceived).

Whereas in classical music women were acknowledged as musicians, in the pop music business of the 70s and 80s, with few exceptions, men were musicians, while women were singers, or sometimes keyboard players, who generally did not improvise, as if they were incapable of creativity. Social conventions of the time discouraged young women from choosing masculine instruments — guitar, bass, drums, any types of horns — and steered them towards tambourines, piano and vocals.

I was serious about music, practising every spare moment, enrolled as a composition major in a Bachelor of Music program at the University of British Columbia. I supported myself by playing in bands at night, though there were few opportunities to play with other women. Playing in all-male bands, however, required that I follow an intricate set of unspoken rules, most of which focussed on silence and complicity. Membership in this boys' club required that I keep quiet about what I saw or heard.

Music days: Genni in The Biz

TRACKS

It is little wonder, then, that when I evoke those years, those journeys, I do so with a jaded eye. But it wasn't all dreary. Most important were the magical moments—those moments on stage that made everything else worthwhile—when in the middle of a solo, the entire band would play a series of licks together, unrehearsed, as if we were, for a moment, tuned into something universal. In his essay, "How Music Lifts us Up," Pico Iyer describes listening to an Eric Clapton concert: "The music was playing him, more than the other way round. In fact, it seemed to be streaming through him—he and his instrument just vessels—and enveloping us all in something beyond the reach of explanations. I didn't have the words for it—I was embarrassed to hear myself saying it—but I didn't care what his religion was or wasn't (or mine, either): this was what the world sounded like when it was unbroken." This is what I fell in love with, not the performances, the stages, the adulation, but the elation once or twice a week, when I suddenly felt connected to something greater, a collective unconscious playing through me. Those moments occurred outside myself; I was carried, lifted—a vessel, as Iyer says—and the moment I tried to grasp it, the sensation would fade like a dream does in the twilight between sleep and awake.

The rest of the time, music was a well-rehearsed performance. We spent hours designing set lists in our rooms, to vary the keys and rhythms. Strung together, songs had to form the lash of a whip that snapped on the last chord of the last song. Each afternoon, we rehearsed choreography for hours, to make it look spontaneous. Everything was rehearsed, including the encore, including the guitar player's final leap into the audience when he had to land on the imaginary X, prearranged, so the follow spot could capture his final frenzy.

And here, a sampling of my other life:

THE BARS

Red Deer, Alberta. We arrive on a Sunday night, after a twelve-hour drive from Vancouver. Stop in front of the Windsor Hotel, a beaten brown rectangle, the lower part streaked with mud, gravel and small stones lodged into the wood—a result of road sandings over many winters. The street is deserted, and the hotel neglected. Two entrances, although defunct, still proclaim in peeling paint: *Men Only* and *Ladies and Escorts*.

"This must be it," one of the roadies says dubiously. He jumps out of the van, and tries the door, which won't open.

The guitar player rolls down the window. "Check for a buzzer."

The roadie feels around the darkened door, gives us a victory sign, and presses the buzzer several times, though we don't hear anything.

OUROBOROS

I look at my watch — 4:34 a.m. — and shiver. It's November, the temperature -10°C. We've come through snow and ice, had to buy chains at Golden to climb Roger's Pass and cross the Rockies.

Presently, a sleepy night clerk opens the door and stares at us, puzzled, as if we have arrived unexpectedly.

"We're the band," the guitar player says.

The clerk nods. "Your rooms aren't ready," he says, crossly. "You can't unload now. Too much noise. *Normal* people are *sleeping*, you know."

We sign in and receive our keys. Nothing is open. We sit in the dim, shabby lobby and smoke cigarettes.

Tonight, we'll be stars.

Later, when we enter the bar to set up our equipment, we're confronted by a huge sign: CHECK YOUR KNIVES AND CHAINS AT THE DOOR. Great, I think. Very reassuring.

We have just landed in one of the roughest bars in Alberta, the legendary hangout of The Rebels MC, later disbanded and reformed as a chapter of Hell's Angels. Ironically, the bikers become our protectors — and mine especially — not allowing anyone to come near the stage to harass or even speak to me.

On Friday night, the bar is tense with testosterone, tables covered in beer mugs — patrons can order 100 at a time, lining up their liquid armies on the red terrycloth tablecloths.

In a bar, at the beginning of the night, people sit around tables, lean against walls, scrubbed lean, combed, smelling of aftershave, body lotion and familiar perfumes, a polite, reserved group of guests invited to the promise of excitement. Then, with each passing hour, eddies of desperation begin to swirl in people's eyes as they search for the fulfillment that has so far eluded them. And finally near closing, if I stare hard enough into the room, I see gusts of unrest. Small-craft warnings. If I close my eyes, I feel the undertow of tension. Bar sales increase. Voices rise, as do the slams of empty glasses on tabletops. On the dance floor, an octopus of arms and legs, hands squeezing buttocks, shirts unbuttoned, dresses wrinkled, hair dishevelled. The bar, in collective degeneration.

The band, too, is in a state of entropy. At the beginning of a tour, we are adventurers crossing an ocean for the first time. Each week, we touch the shore of a new city, hotel, bar, stage — a succession of conquests. The crowd roars. We respond. Soon, however, we begin to wonder who is conquering whom. We are no more / no less than all the bands that inhabit these spaces, reduced to anonymity — projected images of an audience who create us in a collaborative invention; render us static, imprinted on stages — afterimages, mirages.

TRACKS

like travel

Detached, I watch the mating rituals on the dance floor. Far from being the centre of things, performers are always on the perimeters. Looking in. Misfits.

In the Windsor Hotel this Friday night, it doesn't take long for a jealous spat over a woman to go from insult to punch to an all-out bar brawl. Those not involved in the fighting — mainly women — stand on chairs to better see the action.

"Keep playing! KEEP PLAYING!" the manager yells at us, as if we could calm the hurricane of bodies hurtling through the air towards us.

I move as far back as I can, near the drum riser, while the guitarist and roadies try to keep people from smashing our instruments and equipment. Then magically, bikers wrestle their way to the front, parting the sea of arms and legs, and form a tattooed barricade around us. We continue to play, while the police arrive and fill up paddy wagons, while people scurry out of side doors, while the blood is mopped off the floor, while everyone picks up tables and chairs and sets them back down. We continue to play until the dance floor is full and the brawl nothing more than a faint memory.

THE DRESSING ROOMS

No Hollywood decor; no wall-to-wall mirrors framed by round makeup lights, no closets filled with designer costumes, no seafood buffets, no makeup artists, no hair stylists, no easy chairs, no, no, no. This is a basement room, small and windowless. Against one wall, an old couch spills matting from a hole in the armrest. Beside it leans a crooked wooden table with metal legs, covered with an array of half-empty glasses — some from previous nights. Four stacking chairs — the kind one sees in a school auditorium — face a wall, and of these, two are stuck together and used as one. Under the table, a pink plastic bowl overflows with red and green pellets — rat poison. This is a rock-&-roll dressing room; nothing unusual about it. Often, one of the band members leaves a signature: a fork punched into the wall, a smashed light bulb, footprints on the ceiling. On the first few road trips, I complained about these dressing rooms, until a club manager said, "Who do you think wrecks them?"

A TYPICAL 10-WEEK TOUR

Another road trip, this band manufactured by an agent: guitar player from Regina, rhythm player/singer and drummer from Calgary, keyboard player from Winnipeg and me — bass and vocals — from Vancouver. For the past three days, we've been in a Calgary studio, recording album tracks

24

OUROBOROS

for Roxanne, a fifteen-year-old singer, who when she was thirteen had a number one single in Nova Scotia, a province I have not seen in years but will soon, because we have agreed to back Roxanne on a "Maritime tour." *Maritime.* The word evokes oceans, swashbucklers and pirates; the swell of the sea frothing on the wet wooden decks of magical sailing ships. As far-fetched as this sounds, after a multitude of inland bars, a *mari*-time sounds like a better time than we've been having: an oasis after the swashbuckling switchblade crowd in Alberta, where the only froth spews out of taps.

Roxanne's manager needs our band to balance Roxanne in the clubs, because although her voice is strong, her material is mellow. Her father thinks she's too young to sing rock & roll. We'll play the rockers, then bring Roxanne out for two shows a night. Novelty act: sweet little kid singing heartbreak. Roxanne is fifteen going on twelve. It's likely no accident that I've been hired as band leader.

After a couple of gigs in northern Ontario to tighten the band — much like Vegas acts do when they come to Canadian cities to play before their shows open — our first stop is a bar in Fredericton. I recall only the first night, when we announce Roxanne in the middle of the second set, and she steps out from behind the curtain, shy and hesitant. The room noise wanes, and the crowd waits. A power struggle. On first nights, we come out confident and defiant in the first set — to discourage hecklers — a necessary show of strength. Once a heckler begins, there's no stopping it, and by the end of the first set, the manager could be on the phone to the

Music days: Gangbusters

agent, setting up a new band for the next night. We've learned to tame the crowd with familiarity — playing the most simple, basic three-chord songs, with heartbeat tempos — and watching for telltale signs of feet involuntarily tapping out rhythms.

We've already won them over, but now that Roxanne stands here, the crowd is disoriented. She looks too young, too innocent. We begin the intro to her first song, and the dance floor empties. Someone shouts, "rock & roll," others pound fists on tables. Then Roxanne begins to sing. Her voice is deep and husky, incongruous with her child body. The audience hushes.

Such silence. Roxanne's voice, intense, wraps itself around each word. A shiver runs up my spine. Someone in the audience gives a catcall, a whoosh of breaths exhaled, then spontaneous applause. She's won. People filter onto the dance floor, arms entwined, bodies moving, fluid as the voice that guides them.

Through the next few weeks, I try to teach Roxanne the never-ever survival rules of performers:

1. Never go out with someone you meet in a club. These men are not interested in you, only in the performer.
2. Never expose your personal feelings. Performers are created by the audience.
3. Never divulge personal information. The performer has no past, no history, no life other than that which s/he symbolizes.

Roxanne barely listens. She's not even mildly interested in men; she speaks to no one but me and the band members, to whom she says nothing personal. I know, because she has arranged herself to fit into all *my* private spaces. Some mornings, I try to sneak out early for a solitary coffee, but she always awakens and scrambles to join me. As the weeks pass, I feel the role-model constraints tightening. I'm careful about what I say, and I go directly back to the room at the end of each night. Roxanne imitates everything I do. The first time she says "fuck," I'm horrified, not at the word, but at the fact that I've involuntarily taught her something.

I ask the keyboard player to take her out for an afternoon, so I can have a little space, but when he does, I spend the entire time worrying about what they're doing, and when she returns, I question her with the persistence of a prosecuting attorney trying to confirm her guilt. She has weaseled herself into becoming my sole responsibility. I can't wait for the tour to end.

I wish I could recall our trip back to Calgary, the goodbyes, the love affairs that must have occurred in all those weeks, those months, those years. But one trip seeps into another, one love affair into another, none substantial enough to retain.

OUROBOROS

WHAT I CARRIED

Two sets of bass strings, and liquid rubber for speaker tears; scissors, tweezers and nail clippers for grooming; needle and thread (black, white), safety pins and Krazy Glue for wardrobe malfunctions; a small container of talcum powder to remove grease spots; Dristan, throat lozenges, aspirin and Meloids, on which I can sing with strep throat. Trouble is, they only mask the pain. Come Sunday, I can't talk.

ONE-NIGHTERS

There are the blur gigs: ten one-nighters in as many days, from Edmonton to Winnipeg. These are the hardest to recall, reduced to stage times only. The roadies drive and set up equipment, while we sleep in the van, stumble into the venue, and onto the stage, night after night.

The night-time parts, the playing: there's a stage with a carpet black & red, black & blue, black & —, there are five of us in our stage clothes (shiny, satin, silky — all those s-sounds) to go with the lights and the illusions (like women). There are microphones, guitars, basses, drums, sticks, organs — all the male genitalia reproduced in wood and metal — a constant erection. (The females are only passive receptacles in the walls that the males plug into.) There is a room full of people who like music, and/or are lonely, and/or need a drink, and/or are trying to forget themselves. Dancing is foreplay. Watch two people dance. Hear their bodies speak. Feel the tension in the space between them, drawing them closer. We are voyeurs and conductors; lavish orchestrators of fantasies, each set carefully designed to bring this foreplay to a climax. Leave them breathless and pounding for an encore. Magic. Illusion.

In the daytime, if time allows, we roam the streets, ordinary people. Unnoticed, unimportant.

But what do you do for a living? they ask.

What an exciting life, they say.

You are so lucky, so talented, so free, so everything we want, they say.

So much for illusion.

Drinks materialize at the edge of the stage, in front of each musician, increasing as the night progresses until, at lights out, clusters of glasses (empty and full) are all that remains of the band. Ghost markers. Gravestones.

REMOTE LOCATIONS

We fly up to Fort St. John one September and set up in a bar where oil-rig workers spend their ten days off, and most of their money, every month.

TRACKS

What I most recall are conversations with men adamant that after one last tour on the rigs, they'll be returning to their home towns — many in Alberta, but some from as far away as Newfoundland. "Have a nice life," we say to each other when we leave.

I wonder what will happen to the oil rigs, with so many workers departing. Three months later, contracted to return for New Year's Eve, to my surprise, we find the same men, telling the same story, as if they were fooling themselves, or trying to impress us, or perhaps, they simply need to imagine themselves elsewhere in order to make the present tolerable.

Another New Year's gig, this one in Cassiar, a miniscule company-owned asbestos-mining town in the Cassiar Mountains of northern BC. We fly to Whitehorse, then drive the 160 kilometres south through freezing air to a school auditorium, where we set up our equipment. Outside, the town stretches in a perfect rectangle within a picturesque alpine valley between mountains. The open-pit mine at one end of town has since closed, and today Cassiar is a ghost town, having been permanently shut down in 1992, all buildings moved or burned to the ground. And my experience there is ghostly too: an auditorium filled with most of the inhabitants, from toddlers to seniors, the children excited because they have never seen a live band. I break a string, and don't have a replacement. One of the teenagers runs home and pilfers a string from his bass guitar, which I use, then return at the end of the night, knowing how difficult it would be for him to buy new strings.

I wonder if those teenagers recall that night too, now that they've grown and moved away, if we have become a nostalgic ghostly reminder of their youth. We move through our lives as if things will always be there, yet even in one generation, countries change names, towns dwindle and die, buildings crumble, people move away, or die of diseases, overdoses, loneliness.

Twelve years in, when I decided to get off the road, I negated everything positive about the lifestyle, though surely I enjoyed much of it at the time. All that remained was a kind of weariness, in which I imagined the stage set on white sand at low tide. And there we were, keeping time, instruments slung to our bodies. And slowly, as the weeks passed, the tide rose and we tried to ignore the waves that licked our feet. And soon our shins were covered. Our movement sluggish. A constant struggle against the weight as the sea slowly crept up our thighs — a ring of ice numbing. We were still singing, though the ocean's roar was winning, the weight against the chest unbearable. We trudged, inch by inch, deadlocked.

BORDERS

Years after that Maritime tour, a mirage occurs: like that optical phenomenon, in which a displaced image of a distant object appears due to the refraction of light, this one appears due to the refraction of memory. Here in Toronto, currents of laughter rise in the chilly air, as a group of us trudge through snow, heading back to the Comfort Inn after a supper at a Lebanese restaurant a few blocks away. We are slightly hysterical from two days of a writers' conference, of discussions, food and wine. A cutting wind rises, and I pull tight the edges of my hood, my forehead numb and my eyelashes thick with frost. I want to run, but the ground is too slippery for my Vancouver boots.

"Let's go up to Genni's room," someone suggests. "She managed to get the suite." The words condense in a cloud vapour bubble above us.

I'm too cold to talk, fearing my tongue might freeze. I earned my suite, forced to spend the previous night at the Comfort Inn in discomfort due to the teen hockey tournament players who rampaged up and down the halls in drunken hilarity until 4:00 a.m.

In the lobby, in front of the elevator, past faux-Corinthian columns, we stamp our feet to encourage circulation, and quickly push back hoods and peel off gloves. Eight of us cram into the elevator. "Room 413. Bring your own glasses," I call back when I get off at my floor.

I am no stranger to Comfort Inns and their ilk, having spent years on the road as a bass player/singer in rock and blues bands too numerous to name. I walk past the ice machine, momentarily displaced into that other life, down a narrow hallway, its greenish-brown carpet stained by winter boots and pocked with disappointments.

A wave of heat assails me when I open the door to my room. No matter how low I set the thermostat, when I return, it always reads 25 °C, as if reset by a sinister Big Brother or, more interestingly, by a stubborn nurturing housekeeper who believes I might become ill in a colder room. I open the window the three inches it allows, and hang up my coat in the closet by the door.

TRACKS

The suite consists of two hotel rooms connected by an unlocked door. One serves as the bedroom, and the other has been altered to include a kitchenette comprising a tiny counter and sink, a microwave, and bar fridge. A puce plaid hide-a-bed and two matching armchairs bulge in the space. I want to say they are shabby, threadbare, because that's what they conjure: spilled beer and body fluids, slurred words and sloppy come-ons, punches, bouncers standing by the stage — fragments of my other life, the desperate faces, empty eyes, shabby threadbare beings. But the armchairs and hide-a-bed in this hotel are trim and clean. Ugly, but clean. On the wall adjacent to the window stands a small desk. I glance at the phone, its unblinking message button. In front of the window, a small round wooden table and two chairs create a semblance of intimacy. Three Toronto freebie magazines fan across the tabletop.

Within minutes, the gang arrives — an assortment of writers, friends, and acquaintances from across Canada, some of whom I've met at previous conferences and writers' festivals. They carry bottles of wine and Scotch, glasses and buckets of ice. Someone brings a couple of decaf coffee packets and cups, which they place on the counter of the kitchenette. We are eight. Vagabonds, we often reconnect in the most unlikely places — foreign countries, remote towns, our friendships rekindled at will.

"This is great," my friend Gordon says. "How'd you manage to score this?" He sinks into the armchair beside me. He's tall, mid-thirties, amusing.

"I slept with the manager, what do you think?" I say.

"Red or white?" someone yells from the kitchen, holding up two bottles of wine.

"White."

"No, really," Gordon says, and leans into me. "How? I want to know for next time."

"You'll need a bus of teenage boys," I say.

We form a tight garrison with all the furniture. Heap the coffee table with our glasses and cups. Someone sprints to the vending machine and returns with potato chips we eat out of the bags.

Once everyone settles around the room, we chat in twosomes and threesomes for a bit, but soon bond through narrative, the protagonists of stories we recount as one does through the tunnel of time, treating the heartbreaks as maudlin and the humiliating as ridiculous. One-upping each other. My years on the road furnish plenty of narrative ammunition.

The air feels heavy and hot, although the door is ajar, resting against the protruding deadbolt. A knock comes through the wall, and we all shush for a moment, before bursting into laughter.

Music days: Fifty Fingers

Two women now arrive and hesitate at the door, as if searching for someone. I don't know either of them, but I wave them in, and signal for the others to make room. At the conference, they were both reticent, shy probably, around some of the more gregarious writers, and at dinner, they chose to sit at the far end of the table, speaking quietly between themselves.

Gordon stands up and motions one of the women into his armchair. At first, she shakes her head, then shrugs and sits down. "I'm Janet," she says, "and that's my friend Linda."

The other woman — a slender, mid-forties brunette in black dress pants and blue cowl-neck sweater — perches on the armrest.

"Where are you from?" Gordon asks. He slides onto the carpet, and sits across from me, in a semi-lotus position.

"I'm from Nova Scotia," Linda says. "Halifax." She flips her hair behind her ears.

While she continues speaking of her home town, the word *Halifax* circles in my head, in the way words do sometimes, metamorphosing into two, *hali fax*, possibly sea, salt, from the Greek *hal* or maybe *hali* meaning holy. *Seafax, saltfax, holyfax. Halophyte*, the plant that thrives in saline soil. I shake that word worm out of my head, and turn to Janet. "And where are you from?"

"I'm from The Rock," she says, her voice lilting in an almost Irish accent. This sends me off on another word chase, to perilous, winding highways, where I spot signs that read: WATCH FOR ROCK ON ROAD, and envision around the next curve, a trio set up, amps blazing, in an impromptu concert. "Newfoundland," she adds, crossing her legs. Her hair is short and badly cut, her body pudgy in the grey pantsuit, her face the hue of someone who has not spent a lot of time in the sun.

"Where in Newfoundland?" I ask, a dim recollection rising from my ROCK ON ROAD days.

"Corner Brook," she says.

The name whirls me back to an Atlantic tour, to Corner Brook, the streets thick with anticipation for the arrival of the *Oriana*, one of the largest passenger ships in the world, on its final voyage. I took a taxi to the dock, watched it anchor, its 2000 passengers staring out of the eleven decks like miniature figurines in an elaborate diorama roaming the seas, years before the *ResidenSea: the floating city* of only 1000. I was not allowed to board, as if one more body would sink it.

"I bet nobody here's been to Corner Brook," Janet says in a tone that implies there are not a lot of things she can lay claim to.

"I've been to Corner Brook," I say, and everyone turns to me. "I spent a week in Corner Brook. Playing there with a band. Years ago..." I hesitate, trying to extract a memory that hovers beyond my reach: the ocean, laughter, a guitarist dancing in a red dress... "Oh, I've got a hilarious story about Corner Brook," I say, confident it will emerge as I tell it.

"Wait," Gordon says, "I'm going to refresh my drink." He goes to the bar fridge and draws out the chardonnay, while I explain about our five-piece band, and how the guitarist and drummer were locked in a competition for who could bed the most women while on the road. I use a humorous tone, as if recounting a fairy tale: *Both men wanted to win the heart of the princess...* only in this case there were no hearts to win, only the dull hard stones inside these men. I don't say that through years on the road, I had become desensitized and contemptuous of the kind of women I saw night after night in clubs across the country. They were an underclass — groupies — mere conveniences for the men in the band, who were ruthless, ordering them to strip or perform fellatio in the dressing rooms, or sending them off alone into the night after sex. Despite the women's magazines championing sexual *empowerment*, the only power evident in these callous encounters between musicians and groupies belonged to the men. I was incapable of sympathy for women who offered themselves up, who, I now realize, might have been groping for a little fame, a better life, a ticket out of whatever unbearable situation they endured.

"On our last night in Corner Brook, in the middle of our last set, neither the drummer nor the guitar player — the most promiscuous member of the band — had chatted up a groupie, when the drummer looked out into the room and signalled the guitar player over. 'See that girl in the red dress?' he said. 'That's mine.' That's how the guys spoke. Not even a proper pronoun." I pause, listening to the echo of distant heartbeats — my bass in synch to the pounding of drums, to the guitar's blistering licks, to the heat and seduction of music, its intense magnetic field projected onto the musicians, an illusion to which the women flocked, mistaking music for affection. "When we played the last note," I say, "the drummer leapt from the stage, approached the girl's table and collected her. She waited while we packed our instruments into their cases, then followed us to the van outside. We piled in, jostling for position. The girl was drunk and laughing. She wore a red sundress with thin straps that kept slipping off her shoulders. I stared out the window at the stunted vegetation."

"Did the girl tell you her name?" Janet asks.

I shake my head. "She could hardly talk, and anyway, no one asked. We were heading back to the mainland in the morning."

"Didn't the guitar player have a girl?" someone asks. "You said they were in a competition."

"Well, yes, they were, but this one night, the guitar player didn't feel like going through the motions." I say. "The competition had become a burden." I reach for my wine glass and take a sip. It seems incredible that I lived so easily inside that male world, an anomaly, a female musician, when women were mostly singers and tambourine players. I learned to survive in those hives of testosterone by observing, by remaining silent.

"Anyway," I continue, "we drove to the band house, and entered from the basement, where the drummer pressed his hand into girl's back, and led her to his room. No preliminaries. Not even the offer of a drink. The rest of us trudged upstairs, peeled off our stage clothes, and settled to wait out the night. We had decided to drive to the ocean at daybreak, to dip our feet into the Atlantic, to take a step beyond our borders.

"The rhythm guitarist and keyboardist returned to their ongoing game of chess in the dining room, I lay on the couch, watching *Dr Jekyll and Mr Hyde* in black-and-white, and the guitarist paced restlessly around us, stopping in front of the TV, looking over the shoulders of the chess players, though he didn't know how to play. Eventually, he went into the kitchen, and opened fridge and cupboard doors, until he found the makings of a sandwich.

"And then we heard footsteps coming upstairs, and…" All at once, the rest of the story comes flooding back. I take a deep breath. "Oh," I say. "I can't tell this story."

Everyone sits up, or shifts. "What do you mean?" Gordon asks.

"Honestly, it's not such a great story," I say. "And anyway, I can't actually remember it. Really. I'm sorry." A reel begins playing in my head: the drummer came upstairs to say the girl had passed out. He wasn't "into that," he said, and asked the others to help him move her naked body out of his bed. All four men went down. Immobile on the couch, I turned up the volume on the TV and stared at the screen until "O Canada" came on in both official languages. Then snow.

"It was just getting interesting," Gordon says. "That's not fair."

I look at Janet, my face flushing, my heart thudding, back in that other life, when later on, the guitarist came upstairs wearing the red dress; he danced and danced, and we laughed and laughed. I want to ask Janet if she frequented nightclubs, followed strangers to band houses, whether it mattered, one stranger or another, conscious or unconscious, whether she waited for those men's return. I want to say *I'm sorry.*

"What's the matter?" Gordon asks. "Are you all right?"

"Fine," I say, but I'm not all right, suddenly shocked by my own complicity. Silence, too, is a weapon.

I search Janet's face, but she remains impassive.

"I've got a Corner Brook story," she says, and recounts a sad, familiar tale about the gutted fishing industry, and how men all over the island have abandoned families to find work in the oil sands of Alberta. I imagine a landscape of women and children behind curtained windows facing the harbour, waiting for their men, preserving houses as they were, though the men might not return. Waiting, as though their husbands were out fishing in the treacherous waters, or shipped off to war. Waiting as only women can.

"The oil sands," Janet says, "as if Alberta had an ocean."

We're all silent when she finishes. I conjure images of oil spills along pristine beaches, birds slick with tar. The residue, impossible to eradicate.

"That's so depressing," Gordon says, and pours another glass of wine. Then he turns to me. "Come on, Genni," he says. "You must remember that story. We need a funny story."

I shake my head. "What I remember," I say, "is that at daylight, we piled into the van and drove the thirty kilometres to the Atlantic, where we wet our feet." They look at me, disappointed, and someone else begins a story.

I return to my inner screen, where I stand in the dawn light, surrounded by four men, our arms around each other, while a sea rages behind us.

EXPLORATIONS

*What we find outside ourselves has to be inside
ourselves for us to find it.*

— Pico Iyer

BILLOWS

For whatever we lose (like a you or a me)
it's always ourselves we find in the sea.

—e.e. cummings

Those years before I went, *Mexico* conjured a pristine beach at sunset, white sand, rainbow sky, the ocean lapping the shore and there, in slow motion, a wizened old man astride a donkey, saddlebags laden with treasures. Behind him, Eden: verdant with palms, mangroves and fragrant frangipani; populated with coast birds, multi-coloured parrots, albatross and storks; fertile with avocados, ripe grapes and mangoes and any fruit you could desire all year round; abounding with meadows through which flowed crystal rivulets of spring water. This was the Mexico of my imagination, the *me* in Mexico, the *X* in sex, the perfumed luscious paradise of longing to be elsewhere.

The real Mexico my husband Frank and I visit is the sleepy village of Melaque, situated on the Bahia de Navidad, a bay on the Pacific coast, 200 kilometres south of Puerto Vallarta. The half-moon of the bay is three kilometres long, anchored by Melaque at the north end, and at the south by Barra de Navidad — Christmas Spit — a tourist destination, across from which is a privately owned mysterious island with armed guards, a golf course and a luxury hotel — part-cavern, part-villa — built into the side of a cliff overlooking the ocean. No one knows who owns it, but gossip places it in the hands of drug lords, university presidents, minor politicians, or influential families from nearby cities. In the fifteen years these rumours have circulated, no evidence has supported any of these speculations.

Our hotel, Villas Camino Del Mar, is situated mid-point on the bay, all turrets and odd-shaped spaces, as if designed by a drunken architect. At the Melaque end of the beach, a kilometre and a half from our hotel, the three-storey, all-inclusive Casa Grande caters to tourists mostly from eastern Canada. Fishing boats are lined up on the beach in front of it, and at the furthest end of Melaque, an unofficial trailer park has sprung up, housing Canadian snowbirds. In the curve of the bay, children swim in the shallows, huge iridescent dragonflies fluttering around them like buzzards.

We often arrive in early December, before tourist season, when the villagers are going about their day-to-day business, beach deserted, restaurants closed. We can count only on Charly's restaurant on the beach, and the vivacious owner, Licia, who recounts the year's happenings.

Two days before Christmas, the charters arrive in Manzanillo, and the beach in front of Casa Grande teems with umbrellas, lawn chairs and the oiled multitudes in bikinis and Speedos, swimming, playing volleyball, eating and drinking, as if none of this were available at home. On Boxing Day, SUVs of Mexican families drive in from Guadalajara and Colima, and the beach resounds with the shrieks of children, the barks of dogs and the distorted bass lines emanating from boom boxes. On the water, coconuts float by, like decapitated heads, bobbing languidly on waves. Dozens of pelicans congregate, lazy on water. Now and then, they rise up and dive-bomb a passing school of fish.

Not exactly the idyllic scene of my imagination.

However, at the mid-point of the bay, the action is much more subdued, partly because the waves are more dangerous, but mostly because Melaque's small shops are clustered close to the Casa Grande. Each Christmas for twelve years, Frank and I have escaped with a suitcase full of books, oblivious to the splashes in the pool, the green parrot's wolf-whistles, the sweep sweep sweep of brooms in the hallways, the callers with their carts of camarones, ceviche, ice cream, the beeps of car alarms. We read in the shade of palm trees, frond shadows on our thighs—chiaroscuros, skeletons—that sway and waver in the breeze. If I move my legs, the shadows elongate and create the markings of a wild animal. We read, unhindered, from morning till night, when we wander to town in search of food.

Churning tide on Melaque beach, Melaque, Mexico

BILLOWS

This year, we arrive in Melaque two months after the earthquake — an 8.2 on the Richter scale, its epicentre only thirty kilometres away. Extensive damage has crippled the town: the poorest shacks reduced to rubble, the church tower missing, buildings cracked, and the Casa Grande Hotel all bent rebar and buckled concrete, gaping maws where windows once were, everything useful removed and carted away in the aftermath of the earthquake. In front of it, the beach is eerily empty but for the pelicans that glide inches above the water like stealth bombers. It's spooky walking past the dark, gutted buildings, the tiny guardhouse and guard, everything silent but the crickets.

We stay near our hotel, warily watching the thunderclaps of waves on shore, churned and furious, as if the sea were angry to have left some of the village intact. Waves whoosh along the shore from right to left, rumbling past, then curl and fall with a thud. Doors rattle in the hotel. One day a man is sucked out by the undertow, knocked down, and thrown back to shore, his arm broken. I walk along the shoreline in both fear and awe. Sometimes the breakers catch me unaware and almost drag me in, burying my feet in sand. I start swimming only in the pool.

Frank says I see only the anger in the waves, that I'm personifying them. Some days, the waves are ripples. "Come on in," he says, but I'm afraid.

One afternoon, we come upon a small girl sitting on the sand, in front of a collapsed palapa. She resembles a doll, with her bare feet and legs straight out, the ties of her blue jumper forming an X on her naked back. She is completely absorbed in a very glossy flier — a two-page spread of City Shopper Barbie, Winter Weekend Barbie, Ballet Wishes Barbie, Malibu Barbie, University Barbie, Wizard of Oz Barbie, Luncheon Ensemble Barbie, Boater Ensemble Barbie, Cocktail Dress Barbie, Tribal Beauty Barbie. Her desire and longing are palpable, the projections of these consumer women reflected in her eyes, while breakers smash to shore, and fat black butterflies hover above her.

A concerto of crickets accompanies us on our evening walks from the town square, where makeshift church bells summon the faithful to the evening mass in a makeshift church. I wonder how they maintain their faith in the midst of earthquakes and hurricanes. Do they take on some misplaced guilt to exonerate their god?

At night, we often sit on the beach with Salvador, a diver who runs a small restaurant in front of the hotel. A slight man in his fifties, he wears jeans and a white T-shirt which hugs the curve of his stomach. Completely devoid of irony, he tells us that he carves coral and shells into sea creatures. I tell him that coral is the closest in composition to human bone, and is often grafted to a fractured area to help it heal. He picks up his guitar and sings

Mexican love songs about women's healing touch, or volatile moods like those of the sea.

"After the earthquake," Salvador says, "the tide slowly and silently receded, until the bay was empty. It was a frightening thing to see. Can you imagine the uncertainty?" He points to the black roiling water. "We knew something terrible could happen — maybe a tsunami — and everyone ran as fast as they could to higher ground." He points to the hills behind the town. I ask if people stayed in the hotel, climbing to higher floors, but he shrugs. "We all ran," he said. "I don't know if anyone stayed behind, knowing what could happen."

The tide returned, but not as a giant wave. It was much more ominous, emerging in a dark, silent line that continued to advance without breaking — a never-ending tide — until the village was engulfed in three feet of water.

Salvador begins to sing again, and I think about this ocean, the Pacific, its power and thrust. It covers a third of the Earth, and is twice the size of the Atlantic. I think of its underwater mountains and fault lines, rivers and volcanoes — a mysterious undersea life, more powerful than ours above.

Each night, aftershocks awaken us — the concrete bed slab shaking in various directions under us, sending us scrambling outside to wait out the tremors. Many townsfolk are too afraid to sleep in their homes and now sleep outdoors. Waves crash into the shore and the hotel shudders. Flash rainstorms drench us, wind bends the palm fronds, lightning cracks the skies. We've never seen the sea so violent and treacherous. One afternoon, a small Mexican boy almost drowns. Another day, two children. Yet another day, a young man — the sea's moods erratic and impulsive.

Some days, the sea is a polished sapphire. "Come on in," Frank says, but I'm afraid. To me, this ocean is a constant turbulence, though Frank reminds me that dolphins play in the green waves, children bob like corks, sailboats set out, and swimmers lap the bay. But I realize the power of memory: this ocean is the same one I faced in Hawaii, years ago.

My friend Laura and I had come from Oahu, where we'd been for a month, and were now visiting Cynthia, a long-time friend of Laura's. The two of them wanted to take me snorkelling, though I tried to beg off because I am not a strong swimmer, can barely tread water for five minutes.

We drove out to Kealakekua Bay on the Big Island, a marine sanctuary of pristine waters, surrounded by a 100-foot lava cliff, against which the waves hurl themselves. Beneath the water extends a reef of pale purple, pink and white coral, through which swim iridescent tropical fish in brilliant colours. We parked the car and walked across undulating lava for a stretch, because the bay has no road access, then settled in a little cove where the British

BILLOWS

explorer Captain Cook landed in 1778, and was mistaken for a god and revered, then in an ironic twist of fate, was stabbed to death in a skirmish when he returned the following year. A white obelisk memorializes his death.

The tide was going out and had left sparkling pools teeming with exotic sea creatures in the hollows of black lava. I was perfectly happy to look at these, but my friends handed me fins, mask and snorkel and told me to practise for a while.

They secured their masks and fins and walked to the edge of the shore.

"Watch the waves," Cynthia said. "Every seven, there's a lull, and you can get in."

I dutifully watched them count the waves and head into the bay, thinking if we have to find a lull, this can't be a good idea. However, I ducked my head into the water of the shallows and practised till their return. My mask was loose; water seeped in.

A half hour later, someone tapped my back and I raised my face out of the water.

"Ready?" Cynthia asked.

"I guess," I said, feeling not ready at all.

She said, "Watch me," and counted waves, then said, "Now," and I followed her in, slicing through water, my fins propelling me forward, in a way that I had never experienced on my own. I kicked and kicked, luxuriating in the ease of movement. Yellow neon fish swept by my arms. Coral fingers rippled in the deep. A turtle brushed my thigh. I kicked, sliding swiftly through the magical marine underworld. It was the closest I've come to feeling amphibious.

Kealakekua Bay, Hawaii

TRACKS

Abruptly, my snorkel filled with water. I yanked it out of my mouth and raised my head. I was in the middle of the bay, the shore a distant jagged black, white foam exploding against it. Waves towered towards me, over me. I sputtered, the snorkel in my hand, the fins now weights dragging me down. I looked at the waves and at the shore, and knew I could not swim back. I wasn't strong enough. *This is how people drown,* I thought, and everything slowed. *I am going to drown.* I was not panicked, or anxious. I felt an immense calm.

Then I heard Cynthia's voice, "Are you all right?"

"No," I said.

She swam toward me. "What can I do?" she asked.

I did not reach for her, my hands treading water. "Take off my fins," I said. "They're weighing me down."

Cynthia did not argue, but reached below the water, and gently removed the fins. I was completely calm; I recall that moment as if it were happening now. Everything silent, everything freeze-framed.

"I can't swim to shore," I said.

"Yes, you can," Cynthia said. "When you get tired, turn over onto your back. You can float."

I turned over, and abandoned myself to the ocean, floating effortlessly to the surface. Then, I began to kick my feet, and with Cynthia beside me, I swam a little, floated a little, until we reached the shore, where I collapsed, exhausted.

I have been terrified of oceans ever since, though I keep testing myself.

"Come on in," Frank says again, turning his back to the sea, as if to lessen my fear.

I take a deep breath, and gingerly step in, even as a small wave laps my feet. I walk in until I'm fully submerged, and treading water, staring out.

"See?" Frank says. "No problem, right?"

Sometimes the waves surge perpendicular to the shore, and form a chorus line. Sometimes, the ocean's trickery has me believing in the calm ripples, when suddenly a rogue wave rises into a treacherous jade green wall spuming, that curls and furls like a dancer's dress, before plunging in a swirl of foam.

In Melaque, waves break on me, and the undertow sucks me out. Frank jokes and says the calmest sea rises up the second I step into it, like a vengeful god. I still recall that powerful moment in the middle of the bay, the silence, as if the ocean itself had come to a standstill and I was calm and poised toward a certain death.

STROMBOLI

In 1990, while in Hawaii for the summer, I rented a car and headed towards the Kilauea Caldera to see the lava lake inside the Halema`uma`u crater. Volcanoes have always fascinated me, with their unpredictable nature, their fierce reminders that no matter how much we try to shape the landscape, no matter how many gadgets we invent, we are not in control. Nothing equals the power of molten rock breaking through the earth's crust to spill uninhibited across the surface.

I had spent the past week with friends of friends on the Big Island and was aching for solitude. I drove through a cathedral of pines, satin oaks, eucalypti, bushes of strawberry guavas, mangoes, and a gigantic fern forest that made me feel like a Lilliputian. In stark contrast to this were the lava fields — blackened rough lava called *a'a* or smooth thick elephant-skin lava called *pahoehoe*, which stretched for kilometres into the sea. I am inexplicably attracted to deserts and desolate landscapes where nature is unforgiving, terrains familiar in recurring dreams, and this *terra* not so *firma* suited me perfectly.

The eastern side of Kilauea is located in the district of Puna, which, ironically, has the highest growth rate in the county and 45% of the county's subdivided lots, despite the fact that it also has the highest risk of volcanic and seismic activity. Many who live on Hawaii say that Puna is the workshop of the tempestuous volcano goddess, Pele, who continually creates and recreates the island.

Past Kurtistown, on the opposite side of the road, odd things began to appear on the black lava shoulder: an easy chair, a dresser, three suitcases, a birdcage. Then further on, a man squatted, suitcases and boxes in heaps around him. Then a woman, two girls, a couple, more, some half-heartedly sticking their thumbs out when a car drove by. One carried a mattress on his back.

A mysterious exodus, I thought, slowing, then braking. I rolled down the window.

TRACKS

"The lava's coming," a man said urgently. "Taking everything in its path." He paused. "It's not safe. Even The Visitors' Centre has been evacuated. You should turn back."

I thanked the man for his warning and continued up the highway until I came to a *Road Closed — Danger* sign. Having come this far, I was determined to see the lava lake. I backtracked to a side road I'd passed a ways back, and turned down towards the historic Red Road, so called because of its red cinder top, towards the shore. Partway down this road, however, two uniformed park rangers waved me to the shoulder, where I parked behind two other cars.

"There's no car access beyond here," one of them said, spreading his arms, as if to forbid entry to the entire tropical rain forest behind him, and beyond that, the ocean. I got out, nodded, and walked around him, down the road. When I rounded a bend and could no longer see him, I ducked into the forest and headed to the beach. I wanted to see the black tongue of *pahoehoe*, its fiery edges advancing towards me from its molten reservoir three kilometres beneath my feet. I wanted to watch the bubbling lava blaze open the earth. I stood among the tall tall coconut palms of Kaimu Bay and witnessed gigantic plumes of steam as the lava flowed into the sea. Flames rose from the water, as if the ocean itself were on fire.

I had no way of knowing it then, but this was a historic lava flow from Kilauea, which in the next few days engulfed the town of Kalapana, 100 houses and the black sand beach I was standing on at Kaimu. This was not the first time Kalapana had been destroyed. In 1986, a lava flow buried the town, as well as Kaimu and Kaimu Bay, beneath twelve metres of lava. Yet people rebuilt on the same location, in the same trajectory of this volcano's lava flow, which in 2010 flowed once again and destroyed everything in its path. This attraction to danger must be what motivates people to build houses on fault lines, in hurricane zones, in karst topography, at the edge of rivers, below dikes, as if they're testing nature or more likely, themselves. "Danger," Jon Krakauer says in *Into the Wild*, "bathe[s] the world in a halogen glow that cause[s] everything — the sweep of the rock, the orange and yellow lichens, the texture of the clouds — to stand out in brilliant relief. Life thrum[s] at a higher pitch. The world [is] made real."

This yearning for a higher pitch is what makes me seek out another volcano eight years later, Stromboli, situated north of Sicily in the Tyrrhenian Sea. One of the Aeolian Islands — a volcanic archipelago made up of eight islands shaped over 260,000 years by volcanic activity — Stromboli is an active volcano whose written records attest to over 2000 years of continuous eruption.

STROMBOLI

Frank and I are in Venice, ready to board a train for Sicily. I have spent the previous three weeks wandering around Italy, visiting relatives and doing research. Frank joined me in Milan, and we went to Verona to see *Aida* in the splendour of the pink marble Roman amphitheatre. Aida reminds me of my Aunt Ida, enslaved by her devotion to family, by her need to manage everyone's life, Zia Ida, who has entombed herself in the past. We've been in Venice numerous times, and after hours of strolling through its splendours and its crass trail leading tourists like cattle along a shopping artery to Piazza San Marco, we decide to escape to Stromboli, and hastily buy tickets on a night train. My uncle Mario in Rome makes a few phone calls, and books us accommodation for a couple of nights on the volcano.

At 6:00 p.m. we board the *Vagone letto* at Venezia Santa Lucia railway station, laden with cheese, salami, buns, and a bottle of wine. We settle into our sleeping car, and watch the sun shimmer on water as we cross the historic railway bridge over the Venetian Lagoon and head south. After a series of ridiculous incidents which irritate our conductor—getting on without giving him our tickets, pulling down the top bunk instead of waiting for him, borrowing a ladder from the next compartment—we finally lock ourselves in for the night, have dinner and read, while the train slices through Veneto, Emilia Romana, Tuscany, Umbria, and Lazio.

Past Rome, we sleep, and when we awaken, find ourselves in Villa San Giovanni in the region of Reggio Calabria, where the train stops, then in three separate sections snakes into the belly of a ferry that crosses the Straight of Messina. On deck, I stare into the water, imagining myself Odysseus caught between Charybdis the whirlpool monster and Scylla the monstrous creature who devoured six of Odysseus' companions when they ventured near her lair. Our ferry crosses without incident, and I wish we still believed in monsters and supernatural creatures; wish we considered nature's dangers as living and breathing deities.

On the other side, the train slinks out of the ferry, reconstitutes itself into one long snake, and continues on to Milazzo, where we get off, board a bus to the port, and wait for the hydrofoil to take us to the volcano.

Soon, Stromboli rises in front of us—a perfect cone over 900 metres high, black and savage against the cerulean waters of the Mediterranean. Clumps of vapour clouds hover above it, and I think about the 1950s Rossellini film, *Stromboli*, we'd watched back home. Nothing has changed. We could be back in that decade, nearing the volcano's black sand beaches, surrendering to chance, to the earth's volatile moods the camera captured in real-live footage, while the villagers fled into boats.

This active volcano has a particular type of eruption pattern to which it has lent its name: the Strombolian eruption—characterized by explosions of lava and ash at regular intervals. According to an article on the *OurAmazingPlanet* website, based on a study detailed in the July 20, 2010 *Journal of Geophysical Research*, "Stromboli fires when a sponge-like plug, similar to a cork in a champagne bottle, fractures every few minutes due to pressure created by the gas bubbles. This new idea challenges an old theory about what causes Stromboli to erupt, and may help scientists predict how often other volcanoes like it will blow."

We arrive in Stromboli at 4:30 p.m. and are met at the dock by a Mr. Zerelli and his son, who signal us to follow them to our accommodation. The island is far too steep for cars or buses or trains. Dragging our suitcases, we climb the paved footpaths and stairs about a kilometre straight uphill, behind the Zerellis, who walk at quite a clip and never look back. We follow in 38° C, exhausted and panting, to a square, where we stop for a moment to admire the sea and black-sand beaches below us, beside which rise white cubes of stucco buildings. Around 500 residents live on Stromboli year round, in two villages: Stromboli — where we are — to the northeast, and Ginostra to the southwest — a miniscule village with under 50 inhabitants, accessible only by boat or over a perilous mule path. Between them, on the northern flank, is the *Sciara del Fuoco* — Stream of Fire — a sheer black precipice, down which burning lava flows into the sea during explosive eruptions. What an adventure it would be to live here — eyes wide open, ears listening for the subtle shift — the moon, the earth, the sky, the sea, all vivid and *real*, every moment a risk. No time for ennui. I wonder who lives in Ginostra; I wish we had more time, so we could visit there.

After we trudge for another kilometre past the square, we arrive at our accommodation, a tiny cottage in an almond grove. Charming as it appears on the outside, as soon as Mr. Zerelli unlocks the door, we glimpse a dark hovel. In the hallway in front of us, a pile of rubble impedes our passage. Directly above, a shard of sky. I wonder if the volcano launched one of its famous fire bombs, and if we are witnessing its anger. In the room to the right of the rubble are two cots under several inches of dust. Not a sheet, blanket or pillow in sight. Large tropical bugs skitter to the corners of the room and under the cots. Frank and I look at each other and set our suitcases gingerly by the door. The Zerellis act as if they're showing us a five-star hotel.

"Are there any sheets?" I ask.

Mr. Zerelli frowns at me. "I'll have to look," he says, vaguely, not moving.

I step over the rubble in the middle of the hallway (which the Zerellis apparently can't see) and peer into the bathroom, at a mountain of dust, a small cracked mirror, and a filthy glass ledge. No towels or soap. No toilet paper. It's as if the cottage has been completely abandoned or under construction. We could be in that black-&-white film, so similar is the scene when Ingrid Bergman arrives on Stromboli with her fisherman husband to find a crumbling structure, dust, dirt, and the volcano's ashen stamp on everything she touches.

"How about towels?" I ask.

"Towels?" Mr. Zerelli says, puzzled, then sighs and looks at me as if I've asked for something extraordinary. "Maybe I can find an extra sheet," he says mournfully. He gestures to his son, who has remained silent throughout, and the two of them leave.

Frank and I look at each other in disbelief.

"This is a ruin," I say. "In fact, it's worse, because it's a pseudo-ruin." I venture into the bathroom: sauntering along the floor is a gigantic scorpion. I would jump on the toilet seat to avoid it, if it were not cracked in two. I start to laugh hysterically.

"What's the matter?" Frank says, in the doorway.

I point to the scorpion. "That's it," I say. "The scorpion is the last straw. I'm not staying here."

We abandon our zipped-up suitcases, and wander outside into the blinding sunlight, pick fresh almonds, smash them open with a piece of lava, and eat them as we stroll back to the square to inquire about the hike to the top of the volcano.

At the pharmacy, a friendly young woman sells us flashlights, "Because," she says, "this is the darkest spot in the Mediterranean. At night, you will not be able to see in front of your eyes." She listens sympathetically to our sad accommodation story and sends us to Ai Gechi, where, she says, "Good food will help your spirits."

We follow her instructions, up and down lanes, until we find the pots of geranium at the edge of an entrance, and a narrow white stairway to an open-air restaurant, from which we can see the golden lozenges of sun on waves. The owner and cook is a former banker from Trieste — the city of my birth. We quickly bond over this, and when we tell him about our crumbling ruins, he offers us a cottage that he owns and rents. Serendipity.

We collect our suitcases, leave a note tacked to the door for Mr. Zerelli to explain our night flight, and move into the lovely little cottage a few doors down from the restaurant.

During dinner, we gather Stromboli facts: between four and six active vents explode, sending lava and boulders into the air; a significant geological feature of the volcano is the *Sciara del Fuoco*, a big horseshoe-shaped depression generated in the last 13,000 years by several collapses on the northwestern side of the cone; in summer, up to 5000 visitors come to Stromboli; there are six kilometres of black sand beaches; the volcano is 926 metres above sea level, but rises over 2000 metres from the ocean floor; the

Stromboli

locals both revere and fear the mighty power, but would never move. I ask if they feel isolated living here, if they miss anything.

"You cannot miss what you don't need," one of the waiters says. "Even the theatre. Here it's like living in front of a theatre," he says. "We have plenty of excitement."

"But aren't you afraid that you won't be able to get off the island if a big eruption happens?" I ask.

He shrugs, and the others laugh. "We live here all our lives, and the volcano is like a mother and we are the children. We have fear, and we always are watching."

In the morning, we reserve our place for the evening hike, then walk down to the port to check on hydrofoil times, have lunch and make a list of things we'll need for the ascent: bandanas for the dust; two flashlights; food for a picnic; one litre of water each; a change of T-shirt; a pair of pants to wear at the top; two sweaters each, because although in the square it's 38°C, at the summit, strong winds create a stinging chill. In fact, in Homer's *Odyssey*, Stromboli or Aeolia — as it was known — is the home of Aeolus, the keeper of the winds, who welcomed Odysseus and on his departure, gave him a leather bag full of trapped winds — with a warning never to open the bag — so Odysseus could sail home to Ithaca on a gentle west wind. When they were within sight of Ithaca, Odysseus' men, believing the bag was full of treasures, opened it and unleashed violent winds which swept them back to Stromboli and prolonged their journey.

STROMBOLI

At 6:00 p.m. precisely, we stand in the square with eighteen people, ready to follow Giovanni, our guide, up to the volcano. We wear shorts, T-shirts and running shoes, and carry packs that slosh with water. Mine feels like a gigantic boulder strapped to my back. Giovanni is a muscular man, in jeans and a crisp blue-and-white striped shirt. He wears hiking boots and carries a large backpack, probably filled with a first aid kit, water, and whatever else we might need were something indefinable to happen. His hair is black and his clear blue eyes tunnel into a tanned smiling face. He reminds me of my father, who has remained forever forty-nine.

Hiking for me is always an adventure and an exercise in concentration, because I have no depth perception. Born with strabismus — in which the eyes do not focus together — at a time when they didn't do operations for this in babies, my brain shut off the stereo function of my eyes, with the result that I can see out of each of them, but not together. Hence, no depth perception, which in hiking is often what prevents major injuries. Uphill hiking is easier for me, because I can touch surfaces to determine where they are. Downhill hiking is a real challenge, because my brain translates depth in terms of shadow. So, for example, a dark area appears concave to me, and a lighter area appears convex. This means that I can land very hard or not hard enough. Turning an ankle is a perpetual possibility. As well, I can't tell distances, so, for example, if I have to descend from a slab of stone, I have to sit on it and slide slowly down, because I can't judge the distance to the ground. However, if I do it once, my brain retains the information, so that next time, I can easily jump down. All this might sound complicated, but it happens subconsciously. I have never had depth perception: this is how I see the world.

The hike up is divided into three parts: first a tarred road, which narrows past the houses into a trail paved with slabs of lava, then dwindles to a footpath. As it becomes steeper, several of our group turn back, and by the time we reach a lookout point about a half-hour in, we are down to fourteen. From this angle, the top of the volcano appears kilometres away in the sky. The sun blazes from above. I imagine incandescent lava lakes sizzling and bubbling beneath our feet. Giovanni keeps us moving at a quick pace, saying we have to scale the second part before darkness.

From the lookout, we continue up, and now the path shrinks to a mule track winding among caper bushes, tall grasses, lemon and palm trees, flowering cacti, magenta bougainvillea, obsidian talus and scree. Although highly destructive, volcanoes are also a dynamic source of fertility in soils. Volcanic ash breaks down into elements necessary for plants to thrive. Hence the rich tapestry of scorched earth and vibrant exotic plants, the hike more perilous for me, because I have to concentrate on where to put my feet.

TRACKS

Now and then, I stop and turn around, and am startled by how high we've climbed. Below us, white cube houses dot the ankles of the volcano, and beyond it, the blue rippled Mediterranean. Above us, at regular intervals, we begin to see dense black plumes. The higher we climb, the less verdant the vegetation, until all becomes stilted leafless trees, white wisps of grass, singed and ashen against the depth of sky.

At times, we have to scale near-vertical slopes, amid stones and soft volcanic sand. This part is particularly difficult, due to the multicoloured rocks that trick my vision, as well as my pack, which now feels double its weight. I stagger at the end of the line, and Frank takes the water bottles out of my pack and carries them.

Two-and-a-half hours into the trek, dusk begins to fall rapidly. Soon we come to the end of all vegetation and take a short break. All around us are black lava ridges, pumice, and rocks — an eerie charcoal landscape against which, suddenly, a red flare lights up the sky. We ooh and aah, filled with renewed energy, closer to what we've come to see: every fifteen or twenty minutes, for the past 2000 years, four to six vents have erupted in Stromboli's summit crater, creating the ultimate reality-TV show — Earth as angry protagonist spewing its rage high into the sky — a display considered one of Earth's most spectacular amaranthine natural performances.

"We must hurry," the guide, Giovanni, says, "before the dark."

In front of us, the top of the volcano still seems kilometres away. In the dusk, against a dark violet sky, we make out the miniscule silhouettes of people in another group up ahead, walking along the final ridge to the summit, their flashlights twinkling in twilight.

We trek the last section through stones and dense volcanic ash. A bitter wind rises and chills us. I shiver, my T-shirt damp and cold. We all scramble for the sweaters in our packs. Soon, we're balanced on the thin ridge of the old crater, in pitch black, our flashlights the only guides. Below us, the vents begin to flicker and glow, then grow dark. We stare at the ground, climbing now on a narrow ridge which falls at either side of us in steep slopes to the sea.

At the summit, we lean against a ledge of jagged stones. The wind lashes around us — the fury of Aeolus, and though I quickly put on the rest of my clothes, my teeth chatter. About thirty metres in front of us looms the edge of the crater, beyond which extends the darkening sky.

"Put on your helmets," the guide says, and we dutifully do, though I can't imagine what protection they'd be against a lava bomb.

Then a rumbling and hiss begins, like gigantic creatures puffing and panting, and I feel the earth alive and trembling beneath me. How easy to imagine dragons and angry gods readying to expel fire. The vents begin to glow yellow, then a deeper red, lava swirling and bubbling. The rumbling magnifies, the mythical monsters now wild and brawling. One, two, three gasps, then in a sudden burst: incandescent scoria, globs of lava, ash and boulders shoot 200 metres into the air in front of us. None of us speaks, electrified.

In what feels like slow motion, sparks flicker down, and the cooling lava slumps back onto the slopes of the vent, as if the roaring dragons, now subdued, are returning to their fiery dens. As quickly as they erupted, the vents glow red and yellow, the lava lakes recede, then melt into the night, until we are in a dense silence and a darkness so complete we can't see our hands. Above us, a firmament of stars.

Five minutes have passed.

We remain at the summit for an hour and witness three more eruptions, each as magnificent and thrilling as the first. In between, we eat our picnics, and whisper in respectful tones, as if we are on holy ground, our destinies in the hands of a powerful deity. Right now, I can't imagine returning to normal life, so heightened are my senses, so present do I feel.

Soon, Giovanni gathers us for the descent. We follow him to the back of the mountain, down a pumice chute, sinking up to our ankles. Blinded by thick rising dust, we quickly tie on our bandanas.

"Be careful, be careful!" Giovanni repeats every minute or so. "This is a slide zone. Do not venture off the path!" This sounds very dramatic, but I know that landslides and tsunamis regularly occur here. Although I am right behind the guide — who has placed me here because of my vision — in the dust raised by our feet, I can barely see his back, and can't imagine being at the end of our rapid swirling dust storm.

In a half hour, we descend 500 metres down through the slide zone, then the trail becomes a rough steep path we illuminate with our flashlights. I continue down, in reverent silence, both elated and subdued, filled with the awe experienced by all who live on the shores of volcanoes, and who personify these eruptions as the emotions of capricious gods — Pele, Agni, Msaya, Lugh, Vulcan — gods that must be appeased. I replay the final scene of *Stromboli*, when a pregnant Ingrid Bergman scales the volcano, struggling through harsh terrain and fumes of poisonous gas, to collapse at the top. At dawn, she awakens and walks to the edge of the old crater, intent on suicide, until she witnesses the eruptions of lava, the earth's creation. "What mystery," she cries. "What miracle."

CAVES

The cave you fear to enter holds the treasure you seek.

— Joseph Campbell

My fascination with caves has taken me inside many, across three continents. Caves conceal breathtaking formations, underground rivers and poisonous creatures. Both miraculous and nightmarish, they are imprinted onto our collective mythology, ambiguous and necessary.

In Sai Yok National Park, in the darkest chambers of twenty-one limestone caves, live what is believed to be the world's smallest mammal, the Kitti's hog-nosed bat (*Craseonycteris thonglongyai)*, a creature about the size of a bumblebee, weighing less than two grams. Of these caves, the accessible ones are cramped spaces with minute entrances that require lowering oneself feet first, a fact that both excites and frightens me into boarding a train for the five-hour journey from Bangkok.

The other, much more famous/ infamous attraction near the park, is the rail bridge on the river Kwae, and the portion over Wampo Viaduct, built upon long wooden trestles nestled on the cliff side of the riverbank. It is part of the Death Railway, so called because of the 13,000 Allied prisoners and 80,000 Asian labourers who died building this railway from Thailand to Burma during World War II. Ironically, the bridge in David Lean's 1957 Oscar-winning film, *Bridge on the River Kwai*, did not originally cross the River Kwae, but the Mae Khlung. Pierre Boulle, the French author of the novel on which the film is based, was a POW in Thailand, but never saw the bridge, which he wrongly assumed crossed the River Kwae, because the railway ran parallel to it for many kilometres. In a case of life imitating art, when the film's success brought tourists to see the bridge, the Thai ingeniously renamed the Mae Khlung to Kwae Yai (the Big Kwae).

My sister Ileana, her husband Peter, Frank and I arrive a half-hour early at a train station a-chatter with morning crowds, who board train after train, until only a handful of us are left on the platform. Our train is near-empty, and the four of us colonize two sets of facing wooden benches across the aisle from each other. We press against the windows, our bags zipped up on the seats beside us, and gaze out as city skyscrapers yield to shantytowns, rice paddies, sugar plantations, hamlets and villages slashed across the jungle. Smoke rises from piles of burning refuse, and stray dogs half-heartedly chase the train, their mouths open, their pink tongues swinging.

Now and then, a road parallels the tracks, and an air-conditioned tour bus races us, on its way to Kanchanaburi, the last station before the trestle portion of the bridge, where lazy tourists board the train for the seventeen-minute thrill ride. It seems like cheating to me, to not have spent the five-and-a-half hours on the train, on the Death Railway. But we are living in abbreviated times.

At the second stop along the route — and there are six before Nam Tok — I slip in beside Frank and shift his bag next to mine on the bench facing us. A young man in his early twenties climbs aboard and hesitates, surveying us all. His bright orange windbreaker, zipped up partway, exposes a white T underneath. The train lurches forward, and he spreads his legs and balances in the aisle. Although the rail car is practically empty, he slides purposefully into the bench across from Frank and me and stares at us, while he slowly inches closer to our luggage.

"If he's a thief," Frank whispers, "he must be very unsuccessful."

We stare back, half-amused, as the young man nonchalantly rests his elbow on one of the bags, and casually leans on it, like a Charlie Chaplin character in a black-and-white silent movie, his gestures pantomimed and exaggerated. I reach across and pull the bag from under him, almost upending him, murmuring "Sorry," as if my bag were taking up more room than it should. The young man sits up, frowns, and looks at the other bag, which Frank quickly pulls off the bench and onto the floor between his legs. The man now stares away, theatrically, as if in mock annoyance. Then, he stands abruptly, tugs down the edges of the windbreaker, and slides into the bench across the aisle, beside Ileana's bag.

"Twelve o'clock," I say, touching her elbow. "Incoming."

She opens her eyes, and quickly shifts both their bags to the floor between their legs. Now, the would-be thief stands up and stretches, as if his work were done, then heads to the washroom. I wonder what it all means, if we'll discover something missing later on. Frank pulls out *The Impostor* by Damon Galgut, and I look through various brochures on the caves around Sai Yok National Park, thinking about missing things, not in the physical sense, but far beyond it to longing, as if we were shaped by yearning, hollowed by desire, in constant formation, like caves that exist at the edge of cliffs, shaped by wind, on ocean shorelines, carved by waves, on the surface of volcanic islands as lava tubes, in glaciers, tunnelled out by melt-water.

The caves we're heading to, however, are the most common type: karst caves, formed by water dissolving stone, and characterized by sinking streams, depressions, sinkholes, gorges, natural bridges, fluted outcrops, springs, caves, and dry valleys. Karst topography covers ten percent of the Earth's surface, and supplies about a quarter of the world's population with water. It can manifest as rolling hills dotted with sinkholes, or the pinnacles and jagged hills of the tropics. In Italy, I've seen karst caves beneath flat limestone plains, skirting the Adriatic, and on one occasion, beneath a house whose living room had caved in; here, they extend along the riverbank.

Although it sounds fantastic that water could dissolve stone, that's how karst caves form. Rainwater, carbon dioxide and gases from the soil become a weak acidic solution that trickles through cracks in the surface rock and dissolves calcite — the main mineral in limestone, dolomite and gypsum — etching and carving out natural subterranean pipelines that widen with the swirl of more water until eventually, they become caves. To put this in perspective: it takes approximately 100,000 years to create a cave large enough for a human to stand in. Once the cave is established, the drips continue and form *speleothems*, which come in various shapes: *stalactites* — those swords and stone icicles that hang from the cave roof; *stalagmites* — the phallic symbols that sprout from the ground, one drip at a

Lawa Cave, Kanchanaburi, Thailand

time; *flowstones* — the drapes, the calcite on a wall; and *helictites* — growths that twist and turn in various directions, creating delicate formations that resemble flowers, or butterflies, or clumps of coral.

I think of all the caves I've visited, impressed by how fixed and yet precarious are the encrustations. They take centuries to form, making them like living organisms, and, like living organisms, they are altered by touch. The oil from a human hand will disrupt the deposit of minerals and prevent growth in that area. You can kill one through touch alone.

The train lurches to a stop, and from the air-conditioned buses parked at the station, a horde of tourists stampede to board the train. The young man emerges from the bathroom, now badly disguised in a brilliant turquoise windbreaker. He paces up and down the aisle in the most obvious way possible, drawing every eye.

As soon as we reach the trestle part of the bridge, everyone scrambles to the open windows and stares down. Gasps and ooohs fill the air. Without a guardrail, and the tracks hidden beneath the train, we appear to be suspended at the side of a cliff, inching slowly around its curves. Some people lean out, screaming as if on a roller coaster. Others cover their eyes, though they continue to grip the open windows. I imagine the POWs who died building this, the old wooden beams creaking under our weight, the multitude of trains and people who have ridden over them in the past seventy years.

At the next stop, the tourists spill out of the train and retreat to the comfort of their air-conditioned buses, and the young man disappears in the crowd at the station. Was he a decoy, an obvious thief we were all aware of, while a real thief pickpocketed his way up and down the train, as we stared out, the turquoise windbreaker in our sights? I finger the money belt against my stomach.

We check in to our jungle retreat, the River Kwai Resotel, a collection of thatch-roofed Thai cottages, then wander up a path behind the hotel, past a herbal and horticultural garden of medicinal plants, following the hand-painted sign "Lawa Cave" in both English and Thai, up a snaking path to a bamboo grove forming a cathedral ceiling over a steep stone stairway of about 150 steps, up a limestone hill to the entrance of the cave — a small hole we have to duck into.

Lawa Cave is one of the largest limestone caves in Kanchanaburi Province, and consists of various spacious caverns such as the Crocodile Chamber, the Music Chamber, the Throne Chamber and the Curtain Chamber, so named for the spectacular speleothems, shiny and wet, orange-brown through various shades to white. At the entrance, a small sign: *Low Oxygen in the Cave.* I try not to focus on it as we burrow into the cave and the heat increases, and in the cloying, humid air, I fight the urge to turn back.

TRACKS

In the monomyth proposed by Joseph Campbell, in which he examines the hero's journey throughout world cultures, the seventh stage is The Innermost Cave. This is the moment when the hero comes face to face with his/her greatest fear. If he is successful in overcoming it, he is rewarded. For me, this is the fear of being buried alive both physically and metaphorically. Is it any wonder, then, that for as long as I can remember, I have been drawn to caves, testing myself, searching them out wherever I go? And once inside, I am rewarded with the cave's secrets — its past evident in the fragile formations — secrets we can only expose by venturing into the dark, secrets within the caves of our own bodies, secrets like the one my uncle told me years ago, three kilometres inside the earth, in the Grotte di Castellana, in Italy, on my first return since emigration.

I had been riding trains from north to south, reconnecting with aunts, uncles, and cousins I'd never met: my father's family in Udine, Verona, Trieste and Bussolengo; my mother's family in Rome, Bari, Rutigliano, Lecce and Tricase. I had spent the past week in Rome with my uncle Mario, his wife Anna, and my two cousins. Zio Mario is a brilliant man, a walking encyclopedia of cultural and political history. Years after his retirement, he took up the study of sundials and has become renowned in this field, authoring several books and publishing articles in *The Journal for the History of Astronomy*. We had passed many hours travelling to small towns, searching for ancient sundials; to Ostia Antica, Rome's ancient seaport, which is now three kilometres inland due to the gradual silting of the harbour — a ghost town of ruins and treasures, devoid of tourists; to the Church of Santa Maria della Concezione dei Cappucini, where we delighted in the Baroque and Rococo intricate décor that turned out to be fashioned from human bones; and because my uncle shared my fascination with necropoli, to two of our favourite locations: Cerveteri and Tarquinia, where we descended into the underground cities of the dead. You could say we were necropolitans.

Although happy to accompany us on some occasions, Zia Anna was recovering from cancer treatments, and remained in Rome while Zio Mario and I drove south to visit one of my aunts in Bari. On the return trip, we stopped at the Grotte di Castellana, the most famous show cave in Italy, with its Grotta Bianca, White Cave — one of the most lucent white alabaster caves in the world, and one I had never seen.

A *cave* is a hole, a hollow. A way of defining what does not exist. Emptiness and voids. Absence. In Italian, *scavare* means to dig, to hollow out, and can be used metaphorically as well as literally. "Hai scavato un abisso," my aunt once said to Zio Mario, when they disagreed on some point. *You have dug an abyss between us.* (My aunt borders the fine line between dramatic and melodramatic.) A disconnection, longing. The Greek god of sleep, Hypnos, lived in a cave, with his twin brother Thanatos. Silence, a half-death. The Anazazi carved caves out of cliffs, made cities to keep them safe. Sheltering, threatening. The serpent, Python, concealed himself within his cave. Refuge, a mother's womb, tomb.

There, dim violet lights lit our way seventy metres into the earth, barely illuminating the path, first to the largest cave, *La Grave,* The Deep, a cavern fifty metres wide and twice as long, with an aperture through which we glimpsed a fragment of sky. My heart pounded as we continued along various passages, the path narrowing, spiralling down. *Abandon all hope, ye who enter here.* The phrase resounded in my head. Surely, Dante must have descended into this cave, to imagine such strata, these circles of hidden formations, water and stone sculpting for ninety million years. Beyond us, a darkness we could not penetrate. Halfway through the Branch of the Small Paradise, we stopped in the Cave of the Altar, while a guide pointed out the ornate platform that gave the cave its name.

Cave The Deep – Grotte di Castellana

I wondered what would happen if the earth swallowed us there and then. Whether the legends were true, and like Persephone, we would descend into an underworld, invisible to the living, and cross the rivers Styx, Acheron, Lethe, Phlegethon and Cocytus to experience the emotions associated with death: hatred, pain, forgetfulness, fire, wailing. I shivered, drawn to the shadowy passage, the tunnel into the earth.

My uncle drew me aside and touched my arm. "Your aunt is dying," he whispered. Tall, thin stalagmites rose like altar candles against one of the cave walls, and beside us, the guide's elongated shadow flickered, tall and foreboding. "I'm only telling you because this will be the last time you'll see her," my uncle continued. "However, *she does not know. You must not tell her.*"

"Are you sure?" I said, stupidly, knowing he was. How was it possible that they would not discuss this? They were a close couple, affectionate, warm. I searched through memory for clues in conversations with Zia Anna, but found none. Was this white lie to spare her or himself? Avoidance or protection? Both reasons seemed inapt, death too profound to turn away from.

The guide led us out of the Cave of the Altar, into the Corridor of the Desert, a long tall wall extending 450 metres. I squeezed my uncle's arm, not knowing what to say, both our emotions concealed in the subterranean passages of our hearts.

We continued seventy metres down into the earth, to the end, where we filed into an elevator. When we emerged, blinking into the sunlight, it was as if we'd consigned that secret to the depths. We have never spoken of it.

We drove back up to Rome, where I spent my final three days. The night before my departure, Zia Anna and I were sitting on the balcony, when she leaned into me and took my hand. "Listen," she whispered. "I'm going to tell you something, but *you mustn't tell your uncle.*"

Zio Mario was at his office, as Italians are until seven or eight, offices being closed between 1:00 and 4:00 for *pranzo*. I knew what she was going to say, moved at their need each to shelter the other, as if by naming death, they welcomed it.

I was no stranger to this type of reasoning. When my mother was diagnosed with breast cancer in 1969, she was living in Vancouver with my younger brother, while my father was living in Bathurst, New Brunswick — in yet another separation. My mother had a teaching job, two large borzois, and a house in West Vancouver. Rather than tell my father about the diagnosis, she wrote him that she had fallen in love with someone else and wanted a divorce. How could something so devastating and possibly fatal be kept hidden? What did this say about my mother? About her trust in my father's love? Was she trying to spare him the anguish of her illness, or was she afraid he'd reject her because of it? Secrets are difficult to define — the how and why we conceal them, afraid to expose them, as if they were film and could disintegrate in light. Fortunately, my sister phoned my father with the truth, and he flew out immediately. This was another reconciliation, another chapter in their turbulent lives. After the surgery and recovery, my mother sold the house and she and my brother joined my father in New Brunswick, where they remained until my father's death two years later.

My aunt Anna died soon after my return to Canada, and I can't step into a cave without recalling white alabaster walls and my uncle's whisper in the dark.

I tell my sister this, in the safety of the Music Chamber, in the Lawa Cave in Thailand, while the heat presses against us. She has not seen my uncle in decades, was living in Africa when Zia Anna died. I am the only one in our family who returns to Italy often, who scavenges the histories of our relatives, like a forensic anthropologist, searching for proof.

Almost as if bidden, Ileana begins to sing *Dona Nobis Pacem*, and Peter and I join in the round for three or four minutes. We are totally alone in this magical Music Chamber where along one wall the flowstones resemble the pipes of an organ.

The following morning, we hire a boat for the hour-and-a-half ride upriver to the Kitti's hog-nosed bat caves, passing teak forests, banana and sugarcane plantations, water buffalo drinking at the edge of the river, birds, elephants, raft houses nudging the riverbank, and now and then, a barge of rowdy bikinied and swimming-trunked tourists, shouting and singing along to boom boxes.

Past the famous Sai Yok waterfall, we follow the trail to the nearest Kitti's hog-nosed bat cave. Despite their names, these bats are not little kittens with wings, but inch-long bats with pig snouts and a reddish-brown coat. They are named after Thai zoologist Kitti Thonglongya, who, with her British partner John E. Hill, discovered the bats in 1974. These bats are found only in western Thailand and southeast Burma, in limestone caves along the rivers, and number about 5000.

At the entrance of the cave, a small boy charges us the equivalent of fifty cents to rent a flashlight. The cave mouth is a jagged hole in the ground, about half a metre in diameter. A guide hoists himself down first, a young couple follows, then I begin to descend, feet first, bracing myself on the rough ground. Unlike other caves I've visited in Europe and the US, where the temperature drops considerably, in this cave the heat increases with each step down, as if we were close to the centre of the earth. Once we've descended about three metres, the cave widens to one side a little, and I slide into that space. My breath begins to come more rapidly, and suddenly, I'm in Lethbridge, Alberta, in 1991. Hot air sears my lungs as I'm struggling to breathe.

I have the beginnings of a broken heart I'm trying to ignore by spending Christmas in Lethbridge with my friend Dôre and her lover, an aboriginal medicine man named Art. We're inside a sweat lodge we have spent the afternoon constructing, tying the willows, and digging the trench where the stones now glow red and spit searing steam into the air.

The lodge is covered in a plastic tarp anchored with stones, and I'm inside, in a long flannel nightgown, clutching a small towel, which I press flat to the ground, then hold over my mouth and nose in an effort to cool the air before it sears my lungs. I am totally focused on breathing, my heart pounding in my ears, my knees drawn to my chest.

I am afraid of the air, afraid my throat will explode.

Darkness but for the trough of stones, which smolder like red embers moments before water floods over them, creating more steam, more unbreathable air. One by one, voices soar in wordless songs, odd repeated melodies, diatonic scales, yelling and chanting, primal. I take short shallow gulps through the towel, rocking back and forth, thinking *how soon will they open the flap? Am I going to die? How could I have taken air for granted?* And in the darkness, Art calls to spirits, his voice rising, falling, coaxing, until mini-lights flicker around the room, and I wonder if I'm hallucinating from the lack of oxygen, the heat, the hypnotic chanting and the suffocating proximity of those beside me.

There is no epiphany, no sudden glimpse into the future, no conversion of beliefs. However, when the rounds finally end, and the flap opens, I am inexplicably altered, aware suddenly of the mechanics required to breathe, the air, the intake, the rise and fall of my chest.

Later, back at the house, seated at the dinner table, I panic at the closed window. I rise and slide it open, though it's December, the temperature in minus double-digits. And when I leave a few days later, it takes all my willpower to remain strapped into my airplane seat, suddenly conscious of the airtight box. Back in Vancouver, in my car, panic compels me to roll down the window and gulp. For several months, every closed window has me gasping. Something has been awakened: the fear I could stop breathing.

I have never been a fearful person, and I cannot imagine this constriction in my life. And so I create distractions to take with me: talismans — crossword puzzles, word games, Sudokus — anything to keep me occupied, and not thinking about air, which I am doing right there, right now in Thailand, in the Kitti's hog-nosed bat cave.

The guide and the couple in front of me have dropped another metre or so; only their heads and the dim glow of their flashlight are now visible. I stare back up at the opening, that small jagged piece of blue, trying to decide whether to proceed down, when two legs begin to descend, filling the space above me. A shroud. My lungs constrict, the air hot and thin; my breathing shallow and quick.

The word, claustrophobia, from the Latin *claustrum* — meaning "shut in place" — and the Greek *phobos* — meaning "fear" — is based on the fear of running out of oxygen, along with a fear of restriction. Yet in that sweat lodge, I was returned to my primal self, acutely aware of the sheer miracle of breath. Wherever I go, I enter caves to test myself for that ultimate closed space, the lack of air, the hollow inside me, the isthmus between life and death.

RUINS

The man sits cross-legged on a patch of earth, on the russet bank of what appears to be a lake, but is a moat 200 metres wide. He's in his mid-thirties and wears a faded crimson shirt, the sleeves rolled up, and blue jeans. His feet are bare. Pond herons waft in the air in long smooth glides to the surface of still water. Behind the man, a boy splashes waist-deep, collecting pink and purple water lilies. Across the gravel road, an array of vendor stands shimmer in the heat, kaleidoscopic with silk scarves and purses in reds, oranges, and purples, stone amulets to ward off evil, postcards and guidebooks, and rows and rows of water-colour Brahmas who stare out with stony eyes. The man could be a tourist, a bas-relief against Angkor Wat's quincunx pediments, which rise into a sun-lit sky; a tourist resting, perhaps, in the shade of a banyan tree after a day's trekking through temples, but for the large black plastic bag which lies beside him open and overflowing with empty water bottles.

I see him first, as Frank and I round a corner, fanning ourselves with cultural travel guides, our hair semi-plastered to our heads, our feet sluggish in sports sandals, as we search for the rental car and driver who dropped us off at dawn. We have been in Cambodia for four days, exploring the recently proclaimed Eighth Wonder of the World, Angkor Wat, the seat of the Khmer empire when Cambodia was at its height; Angkor Wat, the world's largest religious structure, and the only religious monument to appear on a national flag. Birds circle above us, land in the banyans and *kapots*, whose tubular, aerial roots fall and spread like white hair.

Poised in a wide semi-circle around the man are four teenaged boys in jeans and T-shirts. One wears a light windbreaker. They could be playing a game, so cheerful they are, as each stoops, picks up a stone and hurls it at the man, whose arms rise up, whose hands try to protect his face. The rocks hammer the man's head, his chest, his arms, and legs.

"Stop that!" Frank says, bolting toward them. "What do you think you're doing?"

RUINS

The boys turn, startled, then seeing us, laugh, and continue to pelt the man. I stamp my foot, wave my arms, yelling. One of the boys grows more vicious, adopts a pitcher's wind-up, for better, harder aim. The stone cuts a welt into the man's forehead. Blood seeps into his eyebrow.

"Come on," I say, tugging at Frank's elbow. "Let's just go."

He shakes me off.

Across the street, two shopkeepers emerge from the canopy of their stands. The younger one opens a yellow umbrella against the sun. On seeing the man, they quickly bend to pick up stones. Frank stands in their path. "Stop! Stop!" he says to the two women. "Are you all crazy?"

The shopkeepers stare at us, frowning. The boys turn to the new scene, stones in hand. One of them says, "*He* crazy," nodding to the man. The boy's black T-shirt reads MEGADETH in red letters above a nuclear explosion.

"He's hurt," I say, walking towards the man. I take a tissue from my fanny pack, intending to dab the trickle of blood on his forehead.

The man shrinks from me, shaking his head. His arms cover his face. He begins to wail. The boys laugh and circle him in a crazy dance. I look at the man, who is now curved into a ball, his head low on his chest, his arms wildly trying to deflect the stones.

One of the boys raises his arm and I flinch.

"He possessed," one of the shopkeepers says. "No soul." She picks up another stone, and throws it half-heartedly, so that it does not reach the man, who is moaning and moving his head from side to side in a wanton rhythm.

Temple near Angkor Wat, Cambodia

63

"There's something wrong with him," I say. Japanese encephalitis, I think. All those rice paddies and pigs. Could that have affected his brain? Or war. Or torture. Or family.

The shopkeeper steps back, as if I've struck her.

She shakes her head. "He my teacher once," she says. "But now *preay* ... evil spirit ..." She undoes the knot in her rainbow batik-marbled *sampot*, rearranges and re-knots it around her slim waist. Then, she turns and walks to her stand. The other follows, looking back furtively only once from beneath the yellow umbrella.

"What about karma?" Frank calls after them. "That could be you in a next life."

The shopkeepers continue walking. I turn to the boys.

"This *his* karma," one says. He shrugs and picks up a stone.

Sticks and stones will break my bones... What of these people, stone-faced, stone-blind, stone-hearted? Are their convictions solid as rocks? Is their staunch fear a good neighbour fence or a prison wall? I tread slowly to the parking lot, trying to understand the incomprehensible, my feet raising red puffs of dust, Frank beside me. Stones weather rain, wind and fire. Held in the hand, a stone is a conscience.

Dozens of taxis and buses and tuk-tuks are lined up and waiting for tourists eager for air conditioning and hotel showers. The monument is accessible only on foot, and we are part of a spurt of tourists streaming down the stone causeway half a kilometre long over the moat once filled with crocodiles. We snake past a row of open restaurants with palm-frond

Cow having lunch at head of trail to Kbal Spean, Cambodia

roofs and plastic tables and chairs, dodging restaurant workers' entreaties and vendors trying to sell us the identical guidebooks we hold in our hands. A cow grazes on the corn husks on one of the tables. A massive blue bus narrowly missed us, but leaves in its wake a wall of coral dust. Two boys cycle past.

"Over here," Mr. San calls. He holds the door open for us. He has been our driver since our arrival, an attractive man in his mid-forties with fine bones and a melancholy look in his bleached brown eyes, like a silent film star. Despite the heat, he looks fresh and unruffled in his black trousers and white shirt, sleeves rolled up, unlike how I feel in my dusty white capris and sweaty pink tank top. In the car, I take off my canvas hat and fan it in front of my face. A wisp of hair sticks to one corner of my mouth. Mr. San hands us each a water bottle, then flicks on the air conditioning.

We drive out of the parking complex, past the man who still sits on the ground, a crowd clustered around him. "Why are they doing that?" I say. "That poor man."

Mr. San glances at the scene and shrugs. "Maybe he inherited bad luck. Or maybe," he says, fingering the *lingam* amulet around his throat, "he is possessed by *besach*."

"What's that?" I ask.

"The spirit of person who have violent death."

"There must be a lot of those around here," I say. "You live with this terrible past, and yet you stone a man because you think he's crazy?"

"The man is crazy because a demon has taken him. It is too late for him. We must stone the demon before it comes inside us."

Back at the hotel, while Frank showers, I pick up my travel guide and leaf through it. The Khmer Temples rise glossy in their stone splendor. Demons and deities, defiant, guard the gates. Three-headed elephants. The turreted faces of Brahmas stare out of their cardinal points, seeing all. Laterite stacked into heads, furrowed and pocked by rain and wind. There is nothing about stoning.

However, this hunting and stoning of the possessed is historical, an easy release for our forbidden thoughts and desires. In the biblical tale, a possessed man had banished himself to a tomb, and spent his days crying out and pelting himself with stones so that he was permanently bruised and scarred. The villagers did not dare kill him, convinced the demons inside him were doing the stoning. They chained him repeatedly, put him in ankle irons, but the possessed easily broke out of them all. And so the villagers let him roam — they had a scapegoat, and the madman had his life.

TRACKS

After dinner, the early evening air hangs heavy and humid. I wish I'd worn a dress instead of my jeans. A viscous throng of cars, tuk-tuks and motorbikes clot the street, their headlights like large fireflies in the dark. Hotel marquees announce *Aspara Dancing* or *Happy Hour*, or *Two for One Dinner Free*, signs glittering in multicoloured fairy lights. A motorbike veers towards us on the shoulder of the road. Frank and I stand still while it manoeuvres around us. Dust rises into our faces. I am beginning to regret our decision to walk back to the hotel. A tuk-tuk would have been much cleaner and safer.

We stop at a traffic light and cross onto a wide paving-stone sidewalk. Up past a dilapidated guest house, a restaurant whose sign boasts *We Do Not Serve Monkey, Snake, Rat or Dog*, then a right turn onto Sivatha Street, a main artery flanked with restaurants and shops, past a vacant building whose front is plastered with ads for designer merchandise — Gucci shoes, Armani suits, Prada purses — all in multiple colours. A few doors down, a tiny Internet café is squeezed between a bamboo papaya stand and a digital photo shop, and a little further on, Mr. San is standing by his car, unsmiling, inscrutable. In the open V of his shirt, tattooed letters — a *yantra*, I think, to ward off evil or bullets or grenades. I wonder if he is a soldier, or had been in his youth. Mr. San touches his heart and nods. Goosebumps rise on my arms.

I think about Pol Pot, about the Killing Fields. Almost two million people starved, tortured, murdered. A short drive away, a stone well contains the ghosts of hundreds of mutilated bodies, and behind a glass monument, hundreds of skulls. It seems incredible that no one has been charged, that no one will avenge the dead.

Back home, I'd watched Rithy Panh's chilling 2003 documentary, *S-21: The Khmer Rouge Killing Machine*, set in the Khmer Rouge's Tuol Sleng prison, in which former prisoners, including the artist Vann Nath, were reunited with their captors. What struck me was how stupefied the guards appeared, incapable of comprehending their own atrocities. "If we kill of our own free will," one of them said, "that's evil. But if we are ordered to ..."

The air feels thick and melancholy. I wonder what Mr. San lived through to survive. "They tell us to forget," the artist Vann Nath, said. "But it's like you step in a puddle and get your pants wet. And thirty years later, they have not dried."

Mr. San opens the door of his taxi, and we step in, though we didn't call him. He drives us back to the hotel without speaking. Before we leave, we ask him if he is available to drive us to the Tonlé Lake Biosphere Reserve in the morning, our last day here.

"My mother is sick," he says. "I will see."

I'm worried about my own mother. I draw out my cell phone, check for missed calls or messages, but there are none. Before we left Vancouver, she'd announced yet another impending move, her third in five years. I imagine her packing from morning till night, lifting boxes too heavy for her, not getting enough sleep. Why can't she wait until we return?

In the morning, Mr. San looks haggard and exhausted, though immaculately dressed in pressed black pants and white shirt. He silently leads us outside to his car, then up the main road, past the manicured gardens of restored colonial hotels, away from the throng of buses and taxis, until there are no more guest houses, no western restaurants, no bars. He pulls into a dilapidated gas station, and stops beside a tuk-tuk.

"You go with him," he says to us. "My mother is dead now."

We murmur condolences, unsure about this exchange, but we climb on the tuk-tuk. Mr. San speaks to the driver, then says, "He will take you to submerged forest. I'm sorry."

He steps into his taxi and drives off without a backward glance. The tuk-tuk driver starts up his motorcycle and off we go down the highway for an hour or so. Now and then, boys on motorcycles approach and shout at the driver, who shouts back. Finally, the tuk-tuk turns right onto a side road, where one of the boys awaits. Slowly, the paved road disintegrates into a gravel road, and we find ourselves in the midst of dusty shanty huts with woven walls and tiny roadside stands bloody with the carcasses of animals.

Stone corridors near Angkor Thom, Cambodia

TRACKS

The boy on the motorcycle follows close behind us now. I wonder where we're headed, and take Frank's hand. He smiles reassuringly. Women squat on the ground, shelling nuts, their ragged children scattered around them. Old men stare out of haunted eyes — are they all damaged then? Can any of them escape their own dark history, when victims and perpetrators now live side-by-side, intrinsically linked?

At the end of the road, the tuk-tuk stops, and the driver motions us out. He unhooks the wagon from the motorcycle and gestures Frank up behind him, while I straddle the seat of the boy's motorcycle. We ride for about ten minutes along ridges of red earth, small paths snaking next to Tonlé Sap Lake, until we reach the Tonlé Sap River. There a boat awaits. We hop off the motorcycles and into the boat, where a young man welcomes us in English, "I am Munny, the guide," he says, and turns on the motor.

In the wet season, Tonlé Sap Lake is the largest freshwater lake in South-East Asia, swelling to 12,000 square kilometres through a phenomenon that has the river reverse direction and drain into the lake instead of vice-versa, while in the dry season the lake shrinks to 2500 square kilometres. All this water results in an unique ecosystem — a mangrove forest floodplain, or "submerged forest," as Mr. San put it, rich with 100 varieties of water birds, 200 species of fish, crocodiles, turtle, macaques, otter and other native wildlife. The forest of mangroves form a malachite cathedral ceiling, eerie and dark — a Tolkien landscape, both enchanted and sinister — set against a plated sky.

We continue up the river for about sixteen kilometres till we reach Kampong Phluk, three villages of stilted houses that rise on impressive six-metre stilts that look too thin to support their weight. They are like four-storey buildings with the first two floors missing. We ride past houses, past crocodiles gathered in a makeshift cage on a floating dock. A small pig sleeps in a basket. Up further, an opening.

The sky has begun to cloud, bathing everything in a greyish hue. Slowly the mangroves disappear, and the river widens and widens until all we see is water to the horizon, where it blends into the opalescent sky, with only bamboo poles to delineate the banks. I feel melancholy in this strange landscape, adrift. I reach for Frank's hand, an anchor, home.

Then suddenly, a tune breaks the spell. Munny reaches into his pant pocket, and pulls out his cell phone. "Sorry," he says, and answers it.

I am both startled and amused that we can be afloat, as if marooned at sea, and still have cell reception.

"I will have to go back now," Munny says, replacing the cell in his pocket.

We return as we came, and when we reach Siem Reap, it's still early enough to see Ta Prohm, the temple that represents how the entire complex of Angkor Wat appeared when the French naturalist Henri Mouhot rediscovered it in 1861, while searching for butterflies and beetles. Whereas the other temples are in the process of or have been restored, Ta Prohm, abandoned for three centuries, has been reclaimed by the jungle.

We arrive an hour before closing, when the last of the buses are leaving the complex, the air blue with diesel fumes. The driver drops us off at the west entrance gate. Ahead of us in the distance, the last straggler of a tour group turns a corner, and we find ourselves alone. Above us, four faces are carved into a magnificent stone pavilion, their eyes immutable, all-seeing. The King's eyes. What have they witnessed through centuries? If only they could speak.

Scattered around us lie the ruins of serpent pilastrades, of majestic temples, of mythical creatures — a rust-coloured rubble that, in the late afternoon light, begins to assume sinister shapes. Each massive block has a hole bored into it. A thousand years ago, men carved those holes, passed rope through them, and then attached the ropes to elephants who dragged the stones from the Kulen hills, forty kilometres to the north-east of Siem Reap to their present locations. I try to imagine elephants chained, plodding through the hot dusty terrain, through jungle foliage and flooded riverbeds, their heads bent, their long trunks swirling in the air.

Jungle (Tetrameles nudiflora tree) reclaims temple of Ta Prohm, Siem Reap, Cambodia

TRACKS

A sound begins, like continuous bells chiming, swelling, until I am directly beneath the cicadas in the enormous banyan tree whose roots clutch a temple wall, separating it from the rest of the structure. As I approach, instead of roots, I see white fingers elongated to claws, large monsters, parasites, gripping the temple balustrade, like demons come to challenge the faithful, toppling beliefs, toppling God, Buddha, Shiva, in a powerful show of strength.

Frank has gone on ahead, and I can't see him anywhere. I hurry through a portal, teeter over a collapse of blocks, sharp stone edges digging into my sandals. I find myself in a crumbling courtyard, surrounded by the maws of porticoes made askew by the talons of a sacred fig. A strange rustling sound, then a crack on stone. "Frank?" I call.

I scramble across, and pass through three small temples, delving deeper and deeper into a maze. At every turn, only more rubble, more temples.

"Frank," I call. "Frank, where are you?" I climb up a wooden stairway to my right, and stop at a terrace. The sun is dropping quickly, eclipsed by thick clouds. I hurry along a cloistered walkway until it ends abruptly in another courtyard, bounded by walls with blind doors and square piers filled with dancing *apsaras*. Below me, movement. I jump back as a snake slithers inches from my feet. I draw in my breath and pick up a stone. All around, brown and sandstone blocks are piled high, as if to form an insurmountable impediment, greyish-green with lichen and shadow-like skull reminders of this country's dark history.

"Hey," I hear Frank call, "over here."

My heart is beating hard in my chest. I take deep breaths, then begin to scramble towards him across the mountain of ruins.

Ruins among the jungle at Ta Prohm, Siem Reap, Cambodia

DISCOVERIES

TRAVELS IN MYANMAR
2006 – 2010

As to our vision of creatures and things, what we see is just as much a matter of exclusion as inclusion. There are no innocent gazes.

— Henri Michaux

Previous page photos

Ileana with children in Mindat, Chin State, Myanmar
Chin Woman with N'Kaang clan dot tattoos, Mindat, Chin State, Myanmar
En route from Bagan to Mindat, Myanmar
Intha leg-rowing fisherman, Inle Lake, Shan State, Myanmar
Indein village, Taunggyi, Myanmar
Buddha image in temple, Bagan, Mandalay Region, Myanmar

THE WILD DOGS OF YANGON

Yangon 2006

Pre-dawn, I awaken to the murmur of prayers in a nearby monastery, like an incantation. Then, a polyphonic train whistle blows, and a wild dog howls, joined by two, three, more, a plaintive communal clamour; a train lumbers along the track, tat-tat tat-tat, tat-tat tat-tat, hypnotic as the sole monk chanting a mantra, his voice rising and falling, rising and falling. A gong rings out four times. 4:00 a.m., followed by a two-bar tune through loudspeakers, scratchy and crackling, as if someone has dropped a needle on an old vinyl 78. And the dogs howl. Wild dogs, sad sounds, strange sounds, hungry sounds.

It's December 2006, and this is the first time I have travelled to my sister's space. Ileana and her husband Peter have been living outside Canada since 1982, in Zimbabwe, Botswana, Tanzania, Papua New Guinea, and for the past two years, in Myanmar, formerly Burma, the largest country in mainland Southeast Asia. Ileana is an artist and teaches art, and Peter teaches music and English, but I sometimes think their professions are façades that allow them to travel, and keep them a comfortable distance from the histrionics of our family.

I'm not immune to this either: Frank and I have not spent a Christmas at home in years. Eager to escape conflicts and drama, we've gone in search of all that is foreign and unexpected, yearning to be surprised and enchanted as we were in childhood.

And so here we are in Myanmar. With an area of 678,500 square kilometres, it is bordered on the northwest by India and Bangladesh, on the northeast by Tibet and China, to the southeast by Laos and Thailand, and to the south by the Bay of Bengal and Andaman Sea. Myanmar or Burma? There are varying opinions as to which name to use, although until recently, because "Myanmar" was instituted by the State Law and Order Restoration Council (SLORC) in 1989, what's implicit in the name "Burma" is a political statement against the oppressive military regime. While there, and speaking to the people, however, grey shades emerge. "Burma is the British colonial name," a taxi driver tells us. "We are Mranma."

The name Burma, according to the old *Hobson-Jobson Dictionary* (just to complicate matters a little) "is taken from Mran-ma, the national name of the Burmese people, which they themselves generally pronounce *Bamma*, unless when speaking formally and emphatically... supported by considerable arguments [is the view] that *Mran, Myan*, or *Myen* was the original name of the Burmese people..." First occurring in a manuscript in 1102 as *Mirma*, the name later changed to *Mranma* (the current name in the Burmese language). The confusion seems to arise partly because "mr" in Burmese is pronounced "mee," and often spelled "b," so that Burma and Myanma sound remarkably similar when spoken by a Burmese (as are, indeed, Rangoon and Yangon). Further confusion arises because the name "Burmese" refers to citizenship, while "Burman" refers to the 68% majority ethnic group. We have heard claims that "Myanmar" is inclusive of the 135 national ethnic groups, and claims to the exact opposite: that "Burma" is the inclusive title.

Below the balcony off our bedroom a lush garden of palms and tropical grasses stretches to the road, where in mid-morning a procession of monks in maroon robes advances, from the tallest to the shortest, their feet bare in the yellow dirt. Bougainvillea and hibiscus line a perimeter wall, on the other side of which is a tangled unkempt garden. Indian house crows shriek across the sky, Spotted Doves coo from their nests in the eves, Asian Koels flit across the window, easily identified by their brilliant red eyes, and their distinct call — *Ko-el! Ko-el!*

Ileana and Peter rent a house two blocks from their school, on a dirt road among other houses whose yards are overgrown, as if the jungle has reclaimed them. "They're mostly deserted," Ileana said when we arrived. "Probably built to be rented out, only no one wants to live here." Their house has teak ceilings and banisters, hardwood floors, and ceiling fans they can't use because electricity is intermittent: sometimes an hour a day, sometimes more, sometimes less. They rely on candles and flashlights. The dirt road which runs past their house leads to a monastery and beyond, jungle.

After breakfast, Ileana, Frank and I smear ourselves with 60SPF sunscreen — the temperature 38°C, the air humid — and spend the morning exploring with Simon, a young Myanmar man whom Ileana and Peter have befriended and hire as a driver when necessary. He's 5' 7', slight but solidly built. He wears a button-down long-sleeved blue shirt, *longyi* in tiny blue checks, flip-flops and sunglasses. His English is excellent, as is his sense of humour. He is irreverent about the government, though Ileana told us that he also chauffeurs a retired general.

Yangon, a city of 600 square kilometres — or about five times larger than Vancouver — has a population of four million. While the main roads are paved, many districts are not. Side streets are narrow and potholed; shantytowns exist beside colonial mansions and verdant parks. According to the Yangon Heritage Trust, "Yangon boasts one of the most spectacular urban landscapes in the world. Buddhist buildings of global fame, like the Shwedagon Pagoda, stand amidst mosques, churches, temples and a synagogue. The city retains one of the most complete ensembles of colonial architecture in the world — heritage from the time when Myanmar's former capital was one of the great cosmopolitan trading cities of the world."

We drive on the dusty road in a white, beat-up Toyota, past the security guards of the school where Peter is marking term papers, and over a small wooden bridge, beneath which stretches a filthy polluted riverbed filled with garbage. Mynahs circle above us, mimicking other birds. Crows caw and land on the garbage heaps in the riverbed. Immediately on the other side rises a compound of extravagant mansions, complete with a guard at the gate, the bridge and riverbed, a moat. I think of our mother, how she'd love to renovate one of those.

"Who lives here?" I ask, staring at the majestic, luxurious colonial homes.

"Wild dogs," Simon says, and laughs.

"Are we speaking metaphorically?" I ask.

"It's no joke," Ileana says. "I'll show you later."

From Ileana and Peter's house, Yangon, Myanmar

TRACKS

Simon inches along the deserted grounds. All the houses have bars on the windows and doors. "They are with no one inside," he says. "The soldiers guard the houses only."

Probably an investment that hasn't paid off, I think, as we pass another guard post and leave the compound. "Who could possibly afford these houses, but generals?" I say.

Ileana shrugs. "You think *this* is luxury? Haven't you seen the compilation of photos of the generals' houses on the Web?"

The images have been circling on YouTube, the palatial mansions, the marble and exotic woods, the ornate antique furnishings — certainly these houses pale by comparison.

Wild dogs roam everywhere, unchecked, in packs of ten or twelve. Buddhists do not harm them; some leave out scraps, though Ileana told me that soldiers — while supposedly Buddhists— set out poison from time to time. The feral dogs are mangy and emaciated, both accustomed to people and wary of them. Most people, however, are afraid of black dogs, of their supposed bad luck, which makes them outcasts — the reason, I suspect that Ileana befriended a skin-and-bone one a couple of years ago. When I say "befriended" I mean only that the dog waited outside the gate for her to bring food, and followed her everywhere, five or six metres behind — a distance she maintained. Ileana called her Shadow, and when the dog had puppies, Ileana fed them too. Eventually, all the puppies disappeared but one, which Ileana named Whitey for her light pinkish coat. Shadow had a second litter of pups that perished in the monsoons, when the roads turned into knee-high freshets.

"In some hill tribes, pregnant women eat black dogs to be healthy," Simon says, weaving to avoid the wild dogs that half-heartedly surround the car. A kilometre past the compound, we slowly cross a double set of railway tracks set high on the roadbed. We are on the tracks when a train horn blares, and an old man lowers one arm of the gate behind us, like my grandfather did in Locorotondo, Italy in the 1940s, their house facing the tracks. The train approaches, black and blurry, a mirage in the heat waves rising from steel and gravel.

"Do not worry," Simon says, sensing my anxiety. "Trains go by here every few minutes."

I recall reading that the size of the train makes it appear to be travelling much slower than we think, so it's easy to misjudge the distance. I clutch the door handle, just in case.

"You get used to it," Ileana says, smiling.

I think about danger, how easily it becomes normalized. Like family dynamics, the dangers we encounter each summer, when Ileana returns for a month or so and we embark on a series of hysterical family dinners, where old grudges are resurrected, repeatedly and seemingly without end, as if we were all stuck in a TV sitcom episode which, when we are together, magically begins to replay. We are all, I'm certain, revising our memories, adding spice and fuel for effect. These dinners often end in meltdowns, slammed doors, and tears in the car, which is not happening in Yangon, as we round a bend and come to the main highway, a paved road lined with gigantic billboards, *Nivea Whitening Cream, Midea, 21AD, MAXT, Baby Vita, WELLWOMAN: Intelligent Nutrition for Women's HEALTH, VITALITY & WELL-BEING.* I'm impressed by how literate the English is, when at home, many university students can't put apostrophes and hyphens in the right place. Here, because of the English colonial rule between 1824 and 1948, most of the older generation speaks English. Traffic weaves erratically around us: cars, buses, motorcycles, bicycles and people, all crowding into lanes — yet moving aside when horns beep, in a synchronized swirling dance. I wonder how many accidents occur, and how often, in this city of four million people, whose dusty roads, low buildings and corrugated metal roofs gave it the feel of a small town. The downtown section resembles a 1960s city, with four- and five-storey buildings blackened with soot, their roofs crisscrossed with electrical wires. Tiny outdoor markets sell everything from fruit to flip-flops.

World War II trucks and old car wrecks with left-hand drives from Japan roar past us, though in Myanmar they drive on the right. People cling to the sides of decrepit buses refurbished with wooden slats. Our wreck — a taxi Simon has borrowed for the day — has ripped upholstery, no seat belts or springs, so that each time Simon brakes, we lurch forward. The main streets are paved, but most others aren't. Now and then, a shiny SUV cruises past, or a policeman on a motorcycle.

"At one time," Simon says, "people had a lot of motorcycles in Yangon. Then, one day, the General's children managed to get some and they began to race them. So the General outlawed motorcycles in Yangon. And that's why we don't see any people riding them. Only police can ride motorcycles."

An urban myth, perhaps. More plausible is that the military junta restricted movement to control information and monitor everyone. Most people cannot afford cars, but motorcycles cost about $200.

Ileana says, "I'd like to do a painting of a Yangon street, filled with motorcycles ridden by wild dogs."

We head for Shwedagon Pagoda, the most sacred religious site in Myanmar, and one Buddhists pilgrimage to once a year. A hundred and fourteen acres — about the size of the Vatican — the Shwedagon grounds circle the pagoda, with golden temples housing hundreds of Buddhas, sixty-four stupas and multiple shrines and booths in which people can make offerings. In the centre, plated with 21,841 gold bars, the Shwedagon Pagoda rises like a golden bell, and inside it are enshrined the relics of four Buddhas. At its pinnacle are 5,448 diamonds and a combination of 2,317 sapphires, rubies and topaz. An emerald sits in the middle to capture the sun's rays at sunrise and sunset. And as if this were not enough, rumour has it that even more riches lie hidden inside the shrine.

Four stairways — north, south, east and west — lead up to the pagoda. At the south entrance, we remove our shoes, and climb the 104 steps. The golden Shwedagon rises above us, against a brilliant blue sky. It reminds me of St. Peter's Cathedral. All those rituals and riches, relics and sacrifices.

Conflicting legends attest to the origin of Shwedagon, the predominant one dating back 2500 years, to Prince Siddhartha, who, having recently attained Buddhahood, was offered honey cakes by two merchant brothers from Myanmar. In gratitude, he plucked eight hairs from his head and gave them to the brothers, who on their return to Myanmar presented them to King Okkalapa. When the king opened the chest containing the hairs of the Buddha, the earth trembled, all trees burst into bloom, and jewels fell from the sky. He built the shrine and the pagoda to house the relics.

"Why don't these things happen nowadays?" I muse. "Where have all the miracles gone?" thinking miracles are products of faith, or maybe of the imagination, or as a means to attribute meaning to the inexplicable. I look at the top of the pagoda, but see only the blinding reflection of the sun.

"I've heard," Ileana says, "that during the monsoon when we get cyclones and tropical storms, sometimes jewels do rain from the sky." She smiles.

I imagine the force of winds, rubies and diamonds rolling onto white marble, people scrambling after them.

Walkway at Shwedagon Pagoda, Yangon, Myanmar

THE WILD DOGS OF YANGON

"You must never touch a monk," Simon says to me, as we walk past two monks seated in front of a large Buddha. "And a monk cannot touch a woman, or take anything from your hand."

"Why not?" I ask, though I understand these things are cultural and religious.

He shrugs, then looks to Frank. "*You* can touch a monk, because you are a man."

Frank gives me a playful wink.

I roll my eyes at both of them. Ileana raises her eyebrows in mock shock.

We circle on white marble tiles, and I search for shade, my arms burning. I wish I had some *thanakha* to rub into them. In Myanmar, women's and children's faces are often white with *thanakha*, a lotion made by rubbing the bark of *Limonia acidissima* — known here as wood-apple, elephant-apple, monkey fruit, or curd fruit — against a whetstone. The resulting lotion has been used for centuries as sunscreen, and also to soften and cool the skin. Ileana wears it daily, and she is not sunburned.

We walk in the shade of pagodas and temples. People lie on the ground in front of the Buddha images or stand at small booths to make offerings. Some of the pagodas are encased in bamboo scaffolding, in constant refurbishment. Just like my mother's houses, though here the refurbishment includes a gilding. Shiny surfaces behind which the past is abandoned or concealed. Just like my mother, whose tracks and traces fill behind her.

"I wish Mom could see this," I say to Ileana. She would enjoy the beauty and scoff with us at the wealth of religious monuments everywhere, their existence a paradox in the profound poverty surrounding them.

We watch an offering boat — filled with jewels — going up a pulley to the inside of the scaffolding in the Shwedagon pagoda. I wonder which general is trying to bribe Buddha and whether there are guards here at night.

When we reach the eastern upper platform, Simon stops. "You cannot go inside," he tells us. "Women cannot go there."

Of course, Frank winks again, but less enthusiastically.

I sigh. "What's there? At least tell us what we can't see."

"Inside there is a Buddha who is able to give wishes to people."

"Great," I say to Frank. "I finally get to a place where someone can grant my wishes, and I'm not allowed in."

"It figures," Ileana says.

"We'll go and make a wish for you," Frank says, following Simon.

"You can wish that they'd let us in," I say, uncapping my camera. I snap a photo of them both, wondering what exactly men fear about women's wishes. Ileana and I walk to the gigantic central terrace and settle on a bench. All around, people are sitting quietly, some eating, some praying, some examining the sphinxes and Buddhas and Bodhi trees and temples and temples and temples. Pigeons hop around our feet.

When the sun is overhead, and it is impossible to walk on the scalding white marble, we head off to lunch at a hotel, from where we can see Aung Sang Suu Kyi's house across Inya Lake. I stare through binoculars at the run-down colonial house where she has lived since 1988, when she returned from abroad to care for her ailing mother, and where she has been under house arrest for fifteen of the past eighteen years. The junta was willing to free her if she left Burma, but Daw Suu Kyi knew she would never be permitted to return. Despite the fact that her children and husband were in England, she remained committed to her beloved country, even while her children grew, and her husband died.

Nearby, a hot pink billboard proclaims:

PEOPLE'S DESIRE

Oppose those relying on external elements,
acting as stooges, holding negative views;

Oppose those trying to jeopardize the stability
of the State and progress of the nation;

Oppose foreign nations interfering in internal affair of the State;
Crush all internal and external
destructive elements as the common enemy.

Doesn't exactly leave much room for democracy. Simon points to the top of the buildings. "All high-rises have top floor reserved for the military. Security," he says, a sardonic smile on his face. "On national holidays, they set up all the security there to watch the people. And so, no one wants to live near the top floor."

The windows up there only reflect the buildings facing them.

On the streets, no uniforms, no soldiers are visible, yet I can feel something furtive, threatening — Ionesco's rhinoceros running rampant in the subconscious.

We drive past the University of Yangon, its tall buildings encircled with vines, plants lodged in the cracks, as if being reclaimed by the jungle — a virtual ghost town since the government shut down the university for fear of the reprisals of the 888 pro-democracy protests, when students staged a national demonstration in Yangon, August 8, 1988. Hundreds of thousands marched against the regime, but the uprising ended in a bloody military coup that killed an estimated 3,000 people (although the regime claimed responsibility for only 350 dead). Beyond the barbed-wire fence, nestled within tall grasses, an armoured vehicle points its gun at the sky.

A few kilometres down the road, two white elephants pace at the end of short chains. They are not really white, but pinkish-grey, and when it rains, people tell us, they turn pink. For hundreds of years, white elephants have signalled blessed times, and been objects of reverence and envy in Southeast Asia. Despite their majestic beauty, these elephants look sad, pathetic, restrained as they are — a contradiction, given that they are supposed to be treated like royal children, addressed with the same deference and serenaded with the same music. Here there are no signs of nobility or music. Only the large creatures, restless, at the end of their tethers.

In late afternoon, Ileana leads me to the compound to feed the wild dogs. When Shadow disappeared after her puppies drowned a couple of years ago, Ileana began to feed the puppy Whitey. This year, Whitey has had a puppy of her own, and now Ileana is feeding both. We cross the bridge into the compound, and Ileana says, "The dogs have taken over these mansions. They crawl under the gates and live on the grounds."

As we walk past, gaunt wild dogs rush to the gates and growl, each pack territorial. At the end of the road, we come to a large white mansion, whose yard is overgrown. Ileana calls out, "Whitey!" and the thin white dog emerges from tall grasses, a little puppy at her feet. She is wary of me and growls, but Ileana puts her hand through the iron bars of the gate and pets her. Whitey noses the puppy under the fence, towards Ileana and the bowl of rice-and-dog-food, waiting for the puppy to eat before she eats. She's gaunt and skittish, with large intelligent eyes. It's heartbreaking to see all these hungry wild dogs, living on the grounds of these deserted mansions, as if after an apocalypse.

In the evening, we pack; we're heading out in the morning, flying to several destinations over the next few weeks. The first one, Bagan, is a historical site dating back a thousand years.

Later, I lie in bed, listening to the din of night. Music blares out of boom boxes, night markets open, the air fills with chatter, laughter. How easy it would be to run away, to leave behind the responsibilities of family and duty, of work, and live in the sundrenched tropics, no electronic devices to distract us, our senses open. The time gong sounds hour after hour; dogs bark; a train horn blows, then the train itself hobbles past, its tat-tat tat-tat tired; crickets; another train, quicker tat-tats this time. Train whistle. Gecko tsk-tsking. Train horns again and again. Gong gong eleven times. Train horns. All night, that man at the crossing — a trackman, like my grandfather, and the wild dogs howl.

THE WILD DOGS OF BAGAN

Old Pagan 2006

8:00 a.m. I step out of the hotel bungalow to fenced, groomed, lush gardens, beyond which a yellow desert extends to the edge of the mighty Ayeyarwady River. A chain of blue hills shimmers in the morning sun. Three banyan trees provide all the shade for the restaurant, roots spread, branches clawing the sky. Squirrels run up and down their trunks. Crows shriek, flying back and forth, a murder of crows, whooshing their wings. Whoosh whoosh — the sound of lassos through the air. White-throated babblers hop into potted plants. Frangipani, skeletal grey limbs with single white flowers at the tip of branches. Peter has his binoculars out, and his pencil and bird list: Vinous-breasted starlings, White-throated kingfishers, Great egrets, Ruddy Shelducks, White Wagtails, Grey herons.

At breakfast, served outdoors on the large patio, where all meals are served, on tables covered in white tablecloths, we hear that General Than Shwe — Myanmar's iron-fisted military dictator — is in Bagan, as he often is, to visit the temples and gild the stupas and Buddhas, in a superstitious effort to fortify his power and gain the people's confidence. "When he comes to visit a school," Simon told us the other night, "they have to take the little money for education, and decorate one classroom, so that the General can see it. He spends two minutes there and leaves. Meantime, the towns and villages are suffering for this."

"You won't believe what happened to Peter," Ileana says, nudging him.

Peter rolls his eyes at us, but is a good sport, so he tells us that he was up around 6:00 a.m., wandering about, bird-watching with his binoculars, when in his sights, he was startled by an armed guard staring at him through binoculars.

We all laugh, imagining this unlikely scene, like a slapstick comedy on TV.

"Should teach you to stay in bed until a reasonable hour," I say.

"It was not funny," Peter says, and tells us he quickly lowered his binoculars, and casually walked away.

"Apparently," Ileana says, "the generals are staying at the property next to the hotel."

"You better be careful," I say, smiling.

"They might come and take you away," Ileana says, teasing him, because instead of joining us today, Peter is off on his own birding expedition.

After breakfast, we head out on foot to look at temples all around us, though we could rent a horse-drawn cart or a bicycle. Bagan, formerly Pagan, is an ancient city, the capital of the Kingdom of Pagan between the eleventh and thirteenth centuries, ruled by King Anawrahta. Situated in the dry zone and sheltered from the rain by the Rakhine Yoma mountain range in the west, it spreads for forty-two square kilometres along the east bank of the Ayeyarwaddy. At one time, the plain was dotted with over 10,000 Buddhist temples, pagodas and monasteries. Today, only the ruins of about 2,200 remain, rising above and among the desert vegetation. Of these, the gold and white ones are still in use, while the red brick ones aren't.

It feels as if we are the only people in this vast landscape of red earth, stippled with ancient spires, pagodas, temples. Desert brush and vegetation abound, dirt paths snake from one monument to the other, haphazard and circuitous. Quickly, however, two young boys attach themselves to us — Soe Myint wears a white dusty T-shirt and *longyi*, and Zaw Win an ochre T and jeans rolled up to mid-calf. Both their cheeks are white with *thanakha* and on their feet, flip-flops. In the woven bags around their bodies, the children stash accordions of postcards they sell for 1000 kyat.

"We are guide," Zaw Win says. "We show you."

We follow the children, who explain the history of the ruins, their voices rising and falling, their fingers pointing out this temple or that pagoda. Much of what we learn from the local people and the guides is oral tradition,

Temples of Old Bagan, Mandalay Region, Myanmar

difficult to substantiate through books or websites (as I later discover), but far more interesting. There has been no free press here for decades. The Internet is monitored and blocked. Ileana and Peter get their news every ten weeks in Bangkok, where they go to renew their visas.

"Do you go to school?" Frank asks.

"No," Soe Myint says, "no money for school."

I think about our spoiled children at home, our lax education system, the students' sense of entitlement to good grades, the many functionally illiterate high-school graduates we see year after year. I understand why Ileana enjoys teaching overseas, in countries where education is valued, where students are eager to learn.

A military truck approaches in a cloud of red dust, its open bed filled with heavily armed soldiers, who roam, feral and unchecked, through the countryside, barking orders. We yield to the passing truck. I assume the soldiers are headed for Sinmayarshin Temple, whose golden stupa was regilded in 1997 by Than Shwe, on the advice of his soothsayer; Than Shwe, whose beliefs fuse Buddhism, Nat workshop, astrology, and Yadaya magic rituals — an excellent witches' brew for politics.

As we walk along, a venomous snake crosses the road, a slithering metaphor. We stare at the imprint it leaves in the earth. In this Garden of Eden live thirty-nine deadly snake species, many of which thrive in the abandoned temples of Bagan. Burma has the highest death rate from snakebites in the world — about 1,000 people a year just from Russell's Vipers. Like everyone here, we walk barefoot along dark passages.

"King Cobra," Soe Myint says, keeping a safe distance as the snake slinks away. "See it is thinner in one part and thicker where the head is."

I try to stare at the ground from then on, but not for long, distracted by the splendour of the ruins, the brilliant skeletal frangipani along the road, and then, up ahead, a red carpet stretched to the stairs of a temple, the path bordered by red bougainvillea, and lined with soldiers who stand silent and forbidding in the sun. The children suddenly disappear.

Today was to be the start of the Popa Nat Festival, a festival that goes on for six days, beginning on the first day of full moon in Nadaw, which corresponds to our December. "Nadaw" in Myanmar characters transliterates as "Nat Taw," meaning "Spirit Respect," the veneration of Deities. However, because General Than Shwe is in town, the festival is not allowed.

Wherever he goes, a small army precedes him, clearing the area, setting down red carpets for him to walk on, lining these carpets with soldiers, like wild dogs keeping everyone frightened. He is enemy number one of the people, no matter how much he travels around, pretending to spread goodwill. It is obscene to see the money spent on pomp for this regime, for the new capital Naypyidaw, for the red carpets and lavish houses for the generals, whose disregard and disdain for their own people is staggering.

We walk past the guards and climb the steps. This temple has padlocked iron gates at every entrance except for one — a security measure for the general, though we have seen no one all day. We remove our shoes, step on the red carpet and tiptoe inside, walking anti-clockwise through the long dark passages, admiring the Buddhas, stucco carvings, frescos. As we come to each opening, we find a padlocked gate, and soon we feel as if we're in a maze and have lost all track of where we entered. A motorcycle revs outside, a warning surely. Then a wild dog barks, a man shouts, the motorcycle revs, other wild dogs join in, growing in magnitude until the air reverberates with deep sonorous woofs, yappy small-dog yaps, snarly Rottweiler growls, howls like wolves. A cacophonous canine symphony, an ominous soundtrack. It's easy to imagine we're locked inside. It's easy to imagine a King Cobra slithering toward us. My heart beats faster, recalling the pack of soldiers, the ruthlessness they're known for. My feet speed along the red carpet, and finally, there, the open gate.

We rush out, relieved, and avoiding the red carpet, scramble away from the temple. The soldiers watch us go, their faces impassive.

The two boys now reappear from behind a bush, eager to resume their guiding duties. We turn a corner and find a soldier facing us. Startled, we nod and walk on. At the end of another path, the soldier. The children are wary, furtive. They duck behind bushes. For the rest of the afternoon, no matter where we go, the soldier follows, sometimes surprising us at the top of a temple, his proximity threatening, like the wild dogs circling below. The children disappear whenever he's visible, as if tuned into a collective memory.

"This is biggest temple," Zaw Win says, pointing to Dhammayangyi Temple, a step-pyramid made of identical bricks without mortar.

"Look at the bricks," Ileana says. "They are so precise. According to legend, while this temple was being built, King Narathu would execute masons if he could stick a pin between the bricks. Can you imagine? It was never completed."

"No wonder," I say. "He must have killed all the masons."

This temple has dark long corridors — approximately twenty-five metres per side — surrounding an enormous central core completely filled with rubble. No one knows why, or whether this core is simply a buttress to support the massive building.

We follow the passageways around, tall narrow walls pressing in, and when we get to one end, where small, perforated stone windows let in light, Ileana stops. "You know what this reminds me of?" she says. "Pozzecco."

I stop too, and think about that. Pozzecco is a small village in the north of Italy, where my father's aunts lived and farmed various fields. Ileana and I visited in summers, lay on top of hay wagons, watching the thin dusty road winding among green fields. "You're right," I say. "The paths, the colour of the earth, the feel of this is like Pozzecco." And I recall the magic and superstitions of those happy days, when we slept in the stone mansion, which our great-aunts had convinced us was haunted. "And the ghosts, remember?" I say to Ileana. "Scrabbling in the ceiling, over our bedroom." I look up, where high in the darkness hang hundreds of bats.

"They had silkworms up there," Ileana says. "You didn't really believe the ghost stories, did you?"

"We both did," I insisted, and recalled a memory within a memory — a visit I made to Udine in 1982, to my father's ancestral home where his sister lived, and how, on hearing I was going to visit the great-aunts, she had dissuaded me from staying overnight, citing malevolent ghosts. It grieves me to think how heartless I must have appeared, returning after so long to visit the last two octogenarian great-aunts, with whom my childhood summers are entwined, and not even spending a night with them in that mansion, with its long dark stone corridors, like the ones here in Mynamar, decades later.

"Actually," Ileana says, "I wasn't thinking about that at all. What I was recalling were the times — maybe you weren't there — when I went to Pozzecco with the boy cousins, who would dare me to do crazy things in order to let me play with them.

"One day, I was wandering through the fields with our cousins, and we found an underground passage, a fallout shelter — I think that's what it was, or maybe it was a bunker for soldiers during WWII. It was a cave, really, with a very small opening. Of course, the cousins dared me to go inside." She pauses. "We had been warned about poisonous snakes that lived in crevices in the earth, so naturally, I was afraid. However, I wasn't going to let the boys get the best of me. I was such a tomboy!"

In the winters, when Ileana came to visit me in Rutigliano, she was considered too loud, too rambunctious, an unbroken pony who galloped through the house, broken objects and scoldings trailing behind her.

"And did you?" I ask, though I have no doubt.

"Of course. I was petrified, but I crawled in and it was dark and dank, just like in here, only the walls were closer. I thought a snake would bite me. Oh, they were so impressed with me after that."

"I was definitely not there," I say.

"One of the boy cousins was Australian," Ileana says. "Tulio, I think his name was, and what I remember is his mother, who was everything I wanted in a mother. She took the time to sit with me, to teach me to embroider, and do all the things that little girls did back then. I wanted her for my mother."

Our mother wanted to come on this visit, but we dissuaded her. The oppressive heat would be very difficult for her, and were she to have cardiac trouble, the lack of medical care could prove fatal. As well, with the military presence everywhere, I am glad she didn't come. But I wish my mother could see Ileana as she is here — relaxed and easygoing. And I wish Ileana could see my mother as she is — always restless, always busy. They're both artists; you'd think they would see each other with an objective eye, as they are, and not as they would like the other to be.

Ironically, many of our family dramas are centred on the fact that my mother is in constant movement (we are a testament to displacement), not only country to country, and city to city, and house to house, but also room to room, often — as I like to say — in the middle of a sentence, while my sister or I are baring our innermost secrets (though Ileana and I have learned not to expose ourselves in this way — but that's another story). The result is predictable and infuriating. While I have learned to accept this as *it's not personal; that's the way she is,* my sister treats this as intended disregard: *You never listen. You just ignore me. Why did I even bother coming?* etc., so that by the time the visit is over, she and my mother are tight-lipped and silent.

Ileana vows never to return, though of course she does, the subsequent summer. My mother, too, has this same blackout, and by the following year, when Ileana emails her travel plans, my mother has whitewashed last year's holiday into *Leave It to Beaver.* We are blessed with collective amnesia, all tightly bound by love and drama, in love with love and drama.

I think about the childhood longing for this perfect mother in those years when there was none. Yet we've become who we are because of our pasts. Would we be here, now, in this remote location? Would we have travelled as we have — I for years a vagabond musician on the road — my sister endlessly displaced, returning every year to an altered home? The two of us, rediscovering each other in a foreign land?

In late afternoon, while Peter and Frank play backgammon on the verandah of our hotel, Ileana and I set out with a guide, Lwin Thant, to visit two particular temples: the Manuha Temple and the Nanpauya Temple, both with a colourful history. I carry a journal and a book entitled *Glimpses of Glorious Bagan,* compiled and printed by the Universities Historical Research Centre.

"I will tell you the story that is not in that book," Lwin Thant says.

We follow him to a rather unimpressive structure — a square with a second smaller square as an upper storey.

TRACKS

"This is the Manuha Temple," Lwin Thant says, "built by Mon people for the captured king and queen."

In 1057, when King Anawrahta conquered the Mon city of Thaton, a centre of Indian civilization, he captured the Mon king and queen, and brought to Bagan a large number of the Mon, who were legendary for their artistic and literary traditions. The Mon brought the alphabet, the Theravada scriptures in Pali, and Theravada Buddhism, which today is the dominant religion of Myanmar (89%) and the inspiration for its culture and civilization.

"King Manuka was put in a wooden prison in Bagan. His own people came with him; they were artists and architects, one monk and thirty-two elephants," Lwin Thant says. "The king had one gold ruby ring that he gave to his people to sell to build the temple."

We follow Lwin Thant to the temple. Three entrances shelter three massive Buddha images: the centre one is 14 metres high, while the two side ones are ten metres high. Behind them, stretched across the entire length of the building, lies a 28-metre reclining Parinirvana Buddha. All the statues are too large for the space, their heads touching the ceiling, their arms squished against the walls, built as metaphors for the king who was kept cramped in prison.

"His chest is heavy," Lwin Thant says, pointing to one of the large images, "and he is not smiling — a misery. No one knows how long the king was in prison." Lwin Thant shakes his head sadly, then ushers us to the outer room of the temple where, on a blue tarp, lies a mountain of rice that villagers are measuring into plastic bags for the monks. "When the king came," he tells us, "he had a large bowl built and rice cooked, which he distributed to all the people. So from then on, this represented all those imprisoned by the government. Their family members come to this pagoda to give offerings and to pray to this Buddha for the freedom of their family members." He points to the columns, where under white paint are names and dates, some

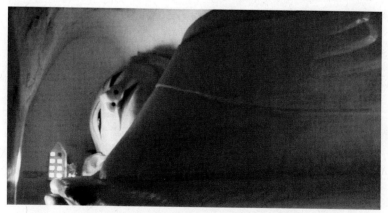

Parinirvana Bhudda, Manuha Temple, Old Bagan, Mandalay Region, Myanmar

of which are visible here and there. "After the 1988 and 1994 time," Lwin Thant says, referring to the uprisings and subsequent military crackdown and imprisonment of hundreds of people, "tourists began to donate money in the name of the political prisoners, and people of the village wrote the foreigners' names all over the walls." He points at the closest one. "When the generals realized this, they had it all painted over in white," Lwin Thant continues. "However, in the rains, the names are coming through."

On our return to the hotel, we are overcome by the fragrant scent of a bush called Nya Hmwe Pann — Fragrant Flower of the Night — which is also the Myanmar slang for prostitutes. We collect Frank and Peter, and walk down a pitch-black road, following the dim circle of our flashlight — not a thought of poisonous snakes — to Mi San Restaurant, an outdoor thatch a kilometre away, where we eat a delicious supper of curried vegetables while puppies lick our feet under the table.

At breakfast, in the morning, we continue to tease Peter about the binocular incident with the soldier, and blame him for our being followed the previous day.

"Careful when you're in the pool," Ileana says.

"Watch out for *the* King Cobra," Frank says.

"Don't go walking on any red carpets," I say.

And suddenly, in the midst of our hilarity, arrives a pack of soldiers flanking a general, who strides directly to our table, as if he's heard everything we've said.

"I am General Soe Naing, Minister of Hotels and Tourism," he announces. He has a large white star on his uniform. "How long are you staying?" he asks, which feels like a trick question.

Our laughter wanes. Our earlier defiance dissipates as the twelve armed soldiers surround our table. Beside me, Frank's face is set. I wonder what consequences there will be if he speaks up. The general looks carefully at each of our faces, but returns to Frank's repeatedly. What could they do to us? I recall the statements we had to sign in order to secure visas, statements that say if we speak against the government, we can be imprisoned. *Oppose those relying on external elements, holding negative views.*

I listen to the murmur of our innocuous responses, to the wind through the banyan tree, the clatter of coffee cups against plates, the chatter of White-throated babblers, the soldiers' boots on stone, the echo of growls, the barks of wild dogs around us, and when the general leans forward, his face in a tight smile, and holds out his hand to each of us, I watch myself from a distance, as if my arm does not belong to me, as it moves up to shake his hand. And the dogs howl.

TERRA INCOGNITA

Trust is a tentative and intrinsically fragile response to our ignorance...

— Diego Gambetta

"It's almost dark," the agent says, furrowing his eyebrows. He wears a black leather jacket and a dark-blue, patterned *longyi*. On his feet, blue rubber flip-flops. In the twilight, his black-rimmed glasses reflect the mountains which hover behind us in various shades of midnight blue silhouettes against sky. He slides open the door of the minivan, and Ileana, Peter, Frank and I step in. Then the agent hands us our passports and tickets, and pats the passenger door, as if it were a water buffalo. "Have a good trip," he says. "I'll meet you here in a few days." He raises his arm, waves, then turns and walks away.

It's December 2007, and in the past week, we have seen only a handful of foreigners — German, Italian, French — no one from North America, possibly due to the travel advisories which recommend against non-essential travel, warn travellers to avoid large gatherings, and point out that freedom of speech and political activity are not permitted here, evidenced in September of this year, when the pro-democracy march led by the monks ended in a brutal crackdown by the military.

In Yangon, at the height of the protests, roads swelled with over 100,000 people forming a cordon around the marching monks, despite the warnings to disperse, in a country where no more than five people can legally gather. Simon told us that trucks full of thugs — some dressed as monks — were stationed on street corners, positioned there to infiltrate the crowd and cause disturbances. Riot police advanced in solid lines, batons banging on metal shields. The crowd armed itself with bricks, no match for tear gas, rubber bullets and live rounds. From the tops of buildings, platoons of armed soldiers pointed guns down into the street. While monks sat and prayed in the shadow of the Shwedagon pagoda, pleading for peace and calm, riot police armed with batons, rifles and bayonets plowed through the crowd, beating dissenters. Some monks tried to flee over walls and were shot. Clashes broke out all over the city. Army units advanced in threatening lines. Soldiers beat and arrested civilians. An estimated 15,000 police and riot troops were on the streets. The government admitted to killing ten people, including a Japanese photographer, whose execution-style murder recorded on a cell phone and broadcast across the world became a contemporary iconic symbol of this government's oppression. According to Al Jazeera, observers said that far more died, but it is impossible to know how many. Thousands of people were arrested during night raids. By the following month, of the 75,000 monks who live in Yangon, few were visible in the streets. "We don't have the strength," one said. "We don't have the weapons. We don't have the freedom."

The minivan pulls out, and we settle back. I'm tense and aware, everything open, everything unfamiliar — the country, the minivan, the two men who speak no English, our destination. We have no way of communicating with anyone outside this minivan, this country, this moment. No cell phones, no internet, no information beyond an itinerary which lists our travel dates. A surrender to trust — something we're not used to back home. In his essay "Can We Trust Trust?" from *Trust: Making and Breaking Cooperative Relations*, social scientist Diego Gambetta claims that trust and uncertainty are codependent. "For trust to be relevant," he says, "there must be the possibility of exit, betrayal, [and] defection." Yet at home, the very possibility of this uncertainty would keep us from climbing into a vehicle with strangers and heading into the unknown. Here, in a country where knowing who to trust is an ambiguous proposition, we are doing just that. If we disappeared tomorrow, who would know? We are easy targets for thieves, carrying *kyat* — no traveller's cheques can be cashed here — and some US currency, although it is illegal for nationals to own it, and hard for them to exchange it unless they have connections, though what exactly constitutes connections, we don't know — a murky territory, without a clear distinction between rulers and ruled. A taxi driver might make a disparaging comment about the junta, then moments later, mention his son is a soldier. We don't stay in government hotels on principle, unwilling to support them, then discover that without government approval, one can't open a hotel. It's all ambiguous, and we are careful with our words.

We planned to undertake this part of the trip in daylight, so we could see the scenery, the climb to the lake. However, our plane has been delayed three hours — no flights in or out — to allow the generals to travel unhindered around the country, their boots pounding red carpets in this yearly expedition of feigned goodwill and devotion, to temples and gilded *stupas,* as if their presence could deceive the Buddha, as if they could gold-foil their way into paradise, while here on earth, their entourages rage state to state, furrowing a trail of fear and misery and death. No one speaks of torture, no front-page exposés, though this year alone, over 900 political dissidents have been locked up in Insein Prison. No world outrage at this insanity. Only silence.

We are in Shan State, headed to Inle, Myanmar's second-largest natural lake. Eight hundred and seventy-five metres above sea level, twenty-two kilometres long, and eleven wide, it is surrounded by high misty blue hills, silk-screened against the horizon. The road is narrow, a one-lane strip, potholed, gravelled, with jagged edges and sheer drops. A fog descends. We travel slowly, quietly, staring out.

In the few weeks before we came, I had read what I could about this country: books and articles of ethnic struggles, bloody history, detailed monstrosities perpetrated by the government upon its people, brilliant political essays in glossy magazines, mediocre web pages of travel agencies, government offices and travellers' blogs. All this seems both inadequate and distant now that we're here, in the semi-dark, faltering on the brim of cliffs, around hairpin curves and switchbacks, the mountainside exotic danger, *terra incognita.* We yield to transport trucks — pre-WWII — to rusted cabs and hooked-nose hoods, to blinding beams in the dismal tracks of tires; swing to one side, manoeuvring past inch by inch, as if in a slow choreographed *pas de deux,* and snake through the obsidian night, our blinded selves awakened to a trance. We don't speak, the air itself charged, and I recall another night, another journey, in Canada this time, on a May 24th long weekend, when on a whim, Frank and I decided to drive to the Interior, almost five hours away.

We left in late afternoon, drove up past Hope, up the Coquihalla Highway with its game fencing to keep wildlife out or maybe us in. In Merritt, with the sun low in the sky, we searched for accommodation among the *No Vacancy* signs.

"It's a long weekend," one motel clerk said, frowning. "Everything's been booked for months." She looked at us and softened. "Give me a minute. I'll make a few calls and see if there's anything available."

We waited in the car. Here and there, clumps of sagebrush huddled in the bare dusty ground. "We could always drive on to Kelowna or Penticton," Frank said, optimistically.

Presently, the clerk came out and handed us an envelope, on which she'd scribbled directions to a horseback riding ranch about an hour away. "Good luck," she said, rather ominously, I thought. We debated whether to search for a restaurant. It was now close to 8:30, and we were both hungry.

Intha leg-rowing fisherman, Inle Lake, Shan State, Myanmar

"There'll be food at the ranch," I said. "I'd rather get there while it's light out." I stared at the envelope. The pencilled directions had us driving for an hour or so to Elkart Road exit, onto a gravel road until we reached a T, then left towards the ranch.

We reached the exit in twilight. We had climbed a steep hill and were now at the top, in the middle of a dense, dark forest. I shivered, and Frank turned up the heat. We hadn't seen a house since we'd left Merritt. The gravel road was rough, as though it hadn't been graded this year. After fifteen minutes more, we came to the T, and found a crude, hand-made wooden sign leaning against a post: "Paradise Lake →," arrow pointing to the right.

"Let's turn right," Frank said. "Paradise sounds a lot better than a horseback riding ranch."

Paradise, yes. I turned right.

In the gathering dusk, we drove for a few kilometres, trying to avoid potholes. Parts of the road were washed away. At one point, we had to skirt a large rock. My hands tightened around the steering wheel. "What if that sign was put there by some thieves?" I said. "What if we're murdered? How do we know there's even a lake here? And why didn't that woman at the motel tell us about it?"

"There's nothing to worry about," Frank said, Zen-like. "You'll see. At the end of this road, we'll come to a magnificent cedar lodge overlooking a pristine lake, the blue of which you never knew existed."

"Sure," I said, trying to keep it light, "or there could be a couple of guys with guns, who will take our car, and if we're lucky, leave us here to die of exposure."

We drove and drove for what seemed like forever, slowly over the uneven ground, the night fallen now, our headlights the only guides. I think of all this, here in Myanmar, half a world away, my stomach clenching, wondering where we are, and why this need to search out the unknown.

TRACKS

And soon, in the shafts of headlights, we glimpse a man here, a woman there, elusive, feet bare, *longyis* knotted at the waist. Some walk, some ride bicycles or trishaws. Ethereal apparitions, coming and going, emerge and fade in the dense dark. Workers returning to their homes after a day in the fields, though we see no lights, no houses, no villages. Most of the country has no electricity, or if it does, it's sporadic, eccentric.

The minivan manoeuvres past villagers, around them, or they manoeuvre around us — all in eerie silence. At times, there are so many, it seems inevitable that we will hit someone, but this never happens. As well as pedestrians, bicycles and trishaws, carts drawn by water buffalo suddenly appear out of the mist in the beam of our lights, either in front of us or coming towards us. And still the driver steers the minivan in and out of this human traffic, in a fluid trance-like motion. A step into another century; crepuscular ghosts dissolving into shadows at the edge of the road.

We thread through darkness for an hour and a half, across a valley twenty-two kilometres long, in the umbrage of mountains, phantoms and banyans scaffolding the sky. None of us speak, as though hypnotized. Then scattered lights. Smoke tinges the air. A village on the lake shore. Dust trails us into Nyaung Shwe, where the streets are deserted, and cooking fires flicker between the wooden slats of thatched huts. Here and there, a generator signals a guesthouse or hotel for foreigners like us.

In front of a crumbling façade, the driver hauls out our luggage, and motions for us to follow, past the darkened building, the peeling paint, the teak colonial door. The night is cool, but our jackets are in the luggage. It seems incredible that only hours ago we were sweltering in the humid 38°C of Yangon.

Two men spring from the shadows, gather our bags and flip-flop around the building. We follow, shivering, our sandals hollow on the wooden planks, until a bare bulb at the rear haloes the shallow draft, the pointed prow — a flat-bottomed boat against a makeshift wharf. The boatmen toss our bags into the skiff, cage them beneath a net as if they might escape. Inside the boat, four wooden chairs await, each with seat cushion and life jacket. Our driver gestures us into the chairs, nodding, his Myanma words soft and encouraging.

The boat sways madly with every footfall. Waves slap wood. When we are settled in, our driver smiles, then turns and walks into the dark.

The boatmen squatting at stern and bow push us off the wharf. The bulb shuts off. Such darkness. The only sound is the splash of oars, the sweep of ironwood, our own elated breaths. And soon our pupils widen to contain the narrow channel cut between mist and tall silhouettes of homes on stilts, night flowing beneath them.

Paradise Hotel, Inle Lake, Shan State, Myanmar

The motor sputters into motion. We skim black water, black night, only the sky a brilliant 3-D tapestry. Now and then, another engine grumbles. Our boatman flicks a flashlight once, twice, three times, catches the eerie shape of a boat ahead or to the side of us. I wonder how we manage not to collide. No one speaks. The air is cold on our bare arms, our thin T-shirts. I carefully pull the life jacket from the back of my seat and use it as a shield against the wind.

I could talk about our destination, the flicker of lights in the distance, the stilt Paradise Hotel in the middle of the lake — the thatched-roof huts connected by a boardwalk; our three days here; the pale-blue, plate-glass lake at 6:00 a.m.; the elephant-grass mats staked into rows in the middle of the lake, bobbing with vegetables, flowers; the magenta hyacinth blossoms drifting languidly in the swishing waves; the floating islands of sugar cane wafting in sun; the woman singing in her house; the narrow waterways between rows of tomato plants; the floating markets of jade, tin, iron, silver; the scent of lavender; the crooked fingers of mountains falling into the lake; the famed Intha leg-rowing fishermen, their cone-shaped nets; the various villages around the lake — these water people: the lotus weavers of Inpawkhon, rhythmic, to the sound of clack, clack, clack; the five blacksmiths of Selkowouen pounding mallets against red hot metal, while an old man fans the fire with chicken feathers; the girls of Nanpan village rolling cheroots below clear plastic bags of water hanging from the rafters to fool mosquitoes or flies into seeing insects larger than themselves; the delicate women in traditional silk or cotton dress — long fitted skirts and tops with modest three-quarter sleeves, rowing boats laden with rice bags, sitting cross-legged, separating threads of lotus, tending the floating gardens; the Phaung Daw Oo pagoda monastery, home to the five miraculous Buddha heads; the Padaung women wearing neck rings which

En route to a Shinbyu ceremony, Inle Lake, Shan State, Myanmar

crush and deform their shoulder bones; Ywama, the largest floating village on the lake — a tropical Venice with its web of canals connecting boardwalks and bridges, splendid teak houses atop large wooden pylons driven into the lake bed; the potted orchids hanging from window-sills; flat boats everywhere: bulging with monks in brick-red robes, laden with fertile mud dredged from the bottom of the lake, brimming with bamboo poles; Indein Creek, which twists and turns under wooden bridges, cuts through sugar cane plantations and rice paddies, its clay banks reinforced with sticks; villagers ploughing, harrowing behind water buffalo, carrying hoes, scythes and baskets; the dirt path past market stalls, past circles of men squatting, up to the ancient stupas, trees growing out of their sides, roots clawing their walls; the small boy who kept us from stepping on poisonous snakes; and back on the lake, the flocks of whistling ducks, the white egrets, the dozens of species of birds, jacanas; floating villages, water people, water.

But what I most recall from this journey comes before all this. We're back in that shallow draft at night, skimming the narrow channel. Suddenly, the sides fall away, and we're out in the lake, travelling swiftly in total darkness, under a dazzling sky. Mist swirls in the air. Here and there, dark clumps of vegetation hover in front of us, beside us, in hazy sculptures the boatmen skirt around. I am thrilled by this remoteness, this total loss of anything familiar, this growing sense of singleness, everything new, all that I know falling away second by second, so that I am simply experiencing the moment, without expectations, abandoned to the mystery unfolding. I wonder if this is how the early explorers felt, their hearts fluttering, their eyes and ears open to the unknown. And as we progress — across the water in the black, black night, I also think about Conrad, and *Heart of Darkness*, and how this journey is a literal journey into darkness, but I have no foreboding, no fear. I am exhilarated by the wind, by the spray of water at our sides, by the brilliant sky and by the darkness itself, which envelops me, ushering me forward.

BURMESE GOTHIC

"Put the camera down," my sister Ileana says, her voice urgent. We're in a taxi — a white Toyota Corolla, circa 1980 — on the way to Yangon airport. She reaches across and gently presses the camera to my lap. "I'm serious," she says. "Last week, a man had his camera confiscated, and now he's in jail." In my mind's eye, I see the monk uprising of 2007, and a Japanese journalist shot at point-blank range.

On every corner, one or two soldiers stand poised, automatic assault rifles slung over their shoulders, as if this were normal. Sometimes, they cluster, four or five, in camouflage gear, chatting, their eyes scanning the crowd. At the stop sign, one stares directly at me as we slowly round the corner, and I quickly avert my gaze, as if my eyes were capable of snapping a photograph.

It's December 2010, only a month since the sham election. Passersby either circumvent the soldiers or are careful to avoid eye contact. I didn't notice such an obvious display of force when my husband Frank and I first arrived a few days ago. This is our third visit to Myanmar, yet the first time the military presence is ubiquitous. Even invisible, however, the military is always present — everyone suspicious of everyone — no one knows who is or isn't an informer.

Bicycles, old rusted cars, and open trucks stuffed with factory workers idle around us. I want to photograph the crowded city streets, the gigantic billboards of radiant young women selling Nivea Whitening Cream set against a background of low-rise buildings blackened with soot and decay. I want to photograph the soldiers' flat expressionless eyes.

We have not been to Myanmar for three years, due to other family commitments. This December, however, Frank and I escaped and came here, to this place one escapes from. I was searching for a respite from all the histrionics of online presences, of endless self-promotions and banal repartee, of the twitterings and YouTubings of tedious, uneventful lives; I was searching and longing for connection — not the superficial wired, cloud,

WiFi connection through technology—but for the physical connection of human to human, and human to the earth itself. I was searching, in short, for utopia.

As well, I had agreed to give a presentation at a conference in the spring, in Udine, Italy, on Ileana's work, specifically on her mixed-media series titled *Displacement, Identity, and Spaces of Desire,* in which I could see our family's story. I wanted not only to discuss with her the influences and inspiration behind the paintings, but also to better understand the effects of displacement as it related to our shared love of travel. The conference brought together Friulan-born artists living abroad, and Ileana and I were perfect candidates. Two of her paintings became covers of my books, so I had perspectives to add to hers. I brought with me colour copies of some of the paintings I planned to discuss with her over the trip.

Ileana's painting *Rupture* depicts a doll whose legs become two railway tracks leading into the distance, separated by water. In the middle we glimpse Ileana's face as a child, over which is a woman metamorphosing into a tree, and on the horizon snowy mountains touch the sky. "I was on the brink of puberty when we came to Canada," she says. "I'm there, at the crossroad, not quite a woman, not quite a child. And the woman/tree is an allusion to Daphne, who was transformed into a laurel by her father when she asked him to save her from being captured by Apollo. The Rockies are Canada, yet another crossroad from one life to another."

And here we are now, and this feels like yet another life. The Yangon airport is packed with domestic travellers. We four are the only Westerners, conspicuous and *other* here, the men in shorts and shirts; my sister and I in pants and solid colours, with our strawberry blonde hair children want to touch, with our bare arms women stroke as we pass. We board the small airplane, and surprisingly, no one asks to see our passports. Based on past experience, I assume they must know who we are and where we're going.

We fly low over whimsically shaped parcels of arable land, over villages and towns, where metal roofs and golden stupas glitter like fools' gold. Here and there, verdant vegetation—an overlay of greens in three-dimensional relief—surrounds pools of water. This year, the rainy season has continued into December, a very unusual occurrence, but one welcomed by farmers. The Ayeyarwady River snakes north of Yangon, muddy and thick, barges and boats floating near its banks. A massive new bridge spans the river, gleaming and monstrous against the rural landscape, against black hills and ridged barren ground. Soon, in the distance, Mount Popa juts out of the mist. At 1500 metres above sea level, the extinct volcano once called "Mountain of Spirits" is the sacred dwelling place of the thirty-seven Nats, or ancestral spirits, and although some urbanites dismiss Nat worship as superstition, outside the urban centres Nat devotion is evident throughout the country in the form of Nat shrines, ceremonial offerings, rituals, legends and annual festivals. In Nat worship — derived from a native form of animism — everything natural is sacred and inhabited by a spirit, so that violation of the natural world is punishable by misfortune.

"Since we have special permission, we can go to Chin state," our guide, Lwin Thant, says in the morning, after we have overnighted in Bagan, "to see Mindat and traditional tattooed women's faces."

Seven of us are travelling in two jeeps: Lwin Thant and two drivers, Soe Myint and Myo Min Tun, and the four of us. We have gasoline and various tools, in case one of the vehicles breaks down. Peter volunteers to go in the open jeep with Lwin Thant and Myo Min Tun, while Ileana, Frank, Soe Myint and I are in the other. I have no expectations other than to enter the journey. I unfold my map and trace the arteries of this country — the Ayeyarwady and the Chindwin rivers — with their boat piers and river jetties along their banks; the train tracks and the roads — veins that carry people and information — reduced to thin capillaries, like the Internet, blocked and monitored. Cruciate railways branch out, tentative arms pointing to select locations — teak forests, ruby mines, oil derricks, river ports — none of them intersecting or connecting, as if designed only to move resources, rather than encouraging travel and linking people. How unlike the railways of my childhood, in Italy, when the only connection between my mother, father, sister and me were the train tracks that crisscrossed the country, that ran in front of our houses, in the valleys behind us, in the midst of Roman ruins, across vineyards and into the downtown cores of cities. Those tracks were lifelines: they carried us to and from each other, bore newspapers and gifts, absorbed the longing of our letters.

In Italy, my sister and I lived most of the year at opposite ends of the country: she in the north, and I in the south. We had no ready access to each other except through the letters exchanged between my grandparents and my aunt, letters about property and taxes and farmlands, with postscripts that said, "Ileana continues to do well at school; Genni is reading *Il Tesoro*." There were other letters, too — the ones from our parents addressed to us. How often I sat at my aunt's desk, writing letters to my father, who was in England or Trieste, and about whom I knew nothing. Unexpected, he would burst in, for a day or two every few months, with toys and stories to charm us. The entire household would awaken as if from a soporific dream: the housekeeper cooked my father's favourite foods, my uncle came home early from work, my aunt bought new clothes, planned dinners and card parties, and for a few days, the house brimmed with happiness and laughter. But when my father left, we all slowly returned to our slumbers. My uncle worked late, the housekeeper tiptoed around, shushing everyone, and my aunt, who I now understand was a depressive, lingered in bed longer and longer each day, the curtains drawn, painkillers slowly dulling her into a somnambulant state. I languished on my bed, staring up at the ceiling, where the shutters cast an intricate mirage, through which I could glimpse shadowy people on the street below. My father was cloaked in political mystery and intrigue. I knew nothing of his whereabouts or doings, but I understood that I could not ask.

We set out for Kanpetlet, only 200 kilometres, yet scheduled to take us approximately seven-and-a-half to eight hours. Such are the roads here—impassable some of the year, and other times forcing a slow and arduous passage. In the rainy season, water cascades down these mountains, creating flash floods and mudslides. Streams intersect the switchbacks. Today, we drive under sunny skies, the air dry and hot, through a varied, patchwork landscape of nuanced colours: green for onions, yellow for sesame, browns for the harvested peanut fields, past *Burmese Gothic*: a lone man irrigating his field with a watering can, a stack of dried palm leaves by the side of the road, goat herds grazing on what little green appears in the yellow ground.

In his *A Handbook for Travellers in India, Burma and Ceylon*, James Haughton Woods, professor at Harvard from 1900 to 1935, devotes only one paragraph to the journey we have embarked upon (albeit by river rather than by road), and it reflects the colonial mentality of the times: "ROUTE 6: Up the Chindwin to Mindat: This trip will take up a good deal of time, and as it contains little of special interest it is not likely to be undertaken by the ordinary traveller…. The river scenery is good but not especially remarkable. Mindat is the headquarters of the Upper Chindwin district, but

Logging truck bound for Chauk, Magway Division, Myanmar

is not otherwise a place of any importance." But is not a place rendered important by association, by human contact? Right now, Ileana and I, who see each other once a year, are in a jeep together, sharing not only this experience, but small bits of our childhood — the missing links, and also those memories that diverge and converge, so that even our *shared* pasts are both strange and familiar. She tells me things that happened to her of which I have no recollection, though I was there.

The jeep slows down at the edge of Singu village, and we both gaze out the windows as the drivers skirt around dogs, and children whose faces are whitened with thanakha. Both jeeps stop at the side of the road, and Lwin Thant jumps out.

"There were here seven colonial houses built by Burmese," he says, "but when the Japanese came, so many during World War II, five of the houses were destroyed by bombs." He hops back into the jeep, and we continue along the dusty road. Men cut and smooth long bamboo poles for fencing. A monk and a novice in red robes barefoot past, nodding to the miniature house with a pointed roof at the end of a long pole — the Nat shrine to Ywa Saung Nat, the village guardian. The road narrows further into a rutted lane, trees cathedral over us, their wide lime-green leaves shimmering in sunlight.

Nature is the best architect. "This is more beautiful than a park," I say.

"Do you remember that little park in Rutigliano we used to go to?" Ileana says.

I scour my memory for a park where she and I are together in southern Italy. All I see is the monument to *Ai Caduti* — the Fallen — in a little square, demarcated by palm trees. "No," I say, "I don't think Zia Ida would have let us go to a park."

"Don't you remember," Ileana says, "how Zia Bianca would take me there, so she could flirt with young men?"

I shake my head. "Maybe no one told me."

"You were always the little angel," she says wistfully.

"I was compliant," I say. "It made life easier."

"Zia Bianca would parade me past young servicemen in crisp uniforms, who would offer me sweets. What a cliché!" She laughs. "But I had always been told to never take candy from strangers, so I refused, while she insisted, saying that the young men were just being nice."

This went on for some time, Ileana tells me, until inevitably someone informed our grandparents that Zia Bianca had been seen speaking to men in the park, and Zia Bianca turned on her, blaming her. "Ileana accepts candy from any young man who offers it. What am I to do? I can't be rude. I *have* to speak to them."

TRACKS

Ileana was spanked and admonished. "It was so *unfair*," she says now, "yet no one believed me. They expected me to do bad things."

I frown, wondering where I was while all this occurred. Could I have been so unaware, or was I sheltered from these events because I was a little younger? Were we so typecast into roles that we inhabited them willingly?

"It's odd what shapes us, isn't it?" I say, understanding a little better our different temperaments.

The jeeps stop in front of a majestic, yellow-and-white mansion, its hexagonal turrets rising in the midst of the saffron sand. "Here we are," Lwin Thant says. Two stone banisters curl to the ground. I can almost hear the twirling ceiling fans, see the ironwood floors and teak ceilings, the bamboo couches and chairs beside carved teak tables, the white-suited men and petticoated women fanning themselves inside.

Instead, we find a three-generational family in a cavernous room, bare but for a Buddha shrine against one wall, an oblong table, its legs in double clay flower pots — the bottom one filled with water — to shield them from termites, a wooden dresser in the middle of the room, a white plastic chair, and two armoires at either side of the teak double doors. "This house," Lwin Thant says, "was built in 1910, during the British occupation." He points to the couple, their daughter, and her two small children. "Their father and mother lived here. They are the relatives." At one end of the room, a four-poster bed frame acts as a shelf for bamboo trays, a half-bag of rice, and a folded blue quilt. Through the open windows, we glimpse lush green grounds, palm trees, and three shiny motorcycles. Lwin Thant leans down and opens a trapdoor in the floor. "After World War II," he says, "bad people would come to rob anyone who is rich, so they have a downstairs to hide."

One of two colonial houses preserved in Singhu Village, Myanmar

BURMESE GOTHIC

On one of the cracked plaster walls hang framed portraits of the dead, watching us: a family of fourteen Burmese; a handsome young man in an ornate chair, a woman standing beside him, her hair in a bun, staring into the eye of the camera, into our eyes. I try to imagine how she may have felt living here 100 years ago, when Burma was one of the richest, most developed countries in Southeast Asia, glad she is not here to see the spectre it has become. Journeying to the distant past, however, is an act of imagination, a re-envisioning of the unknown. It's difficult enough to revisit one's own past, those places idealized in memory.

In 1983, eleven years after my father's death, I returned to Italy for the first time since leaving in 1960, to a country in turmoil. The Years of Lead (*Anni di Piombo*) — between 1969 and 1982 — had left nearly 2,000 people murdered in acts of political violence implemented by both right- and left-wing paramilitary groups: The Bologna Massacre was carried out by The Nuclei Armati Rivoluzionari (NAR); Carlo Della Chiesa, head of counter-terrorism, was assassinated by the Mafia; Aldo Moro was kidnapped and murdered by the Red Brigades. A few weeks before my arrival, a young woman had been kidnapped. Police in blue uniforms stood in pairs on street corners, eyeing cars and passersby, their hands on the triggers of their guns. In Rome, it was impossible to travel far without coming across police roadblocks and checkpoints. Everyone was nervous and suspicious of the heavily armed police, who now had carte blanche to stop, arrest and detain without warrants. "We are reduced to a police state," my uncle said. I thought about Mussolini's Black Shirts and how quickly protection can become oppression. We are destined, it seems, to learn nothing from our history. How quickly we relinquish power to others in the name of security.

I took a train north to Pozzecco, a village a few kilometres out of Udine, to visit my father's beloved maiden aunts. Ileana and I had spent many summers there as children, and I was anxious to revisit these memory palaces — both mine and my father's. The old house was majestic, much like this one, decades later in another country, a testament to the building itself, and to its inhabitants' care. My father and his two siblings had inherited the Pozzecco house, with the stipulation that the old aunts would live out their lives there, and these aunts kept a wing of the house exactly as it had been many years before, when my father and mother had lived there for a brief period.

I am not attached to houses, and with the exception of our current home, have moved every three or four years throughout my life. Perhaps this comes from not having a physical home in Italy while growing up, and searching even then for that unreal space called utopia, a nostalgic mirror that would situate me within a childhood family home. In Canada, my father longed to return to some imagined place, to some connection, a memory perhaps, restless and unsettled. He travelled back and forth across lands and oceans, yearning in desire. In his poem "Ulysses" Tennyson says, "All experience is an arch wherethrough / Gleams that untravelled world, whose margin fades /For ever and for ever when I move." I used to think my father was Ulysses, searching for the untravelled world; I used to think he chose the distance: I used to think we were the ever-fading margin, being no strangers to travel, my sister and I. As far as I can remember, and before that, we have been travelling to and from each other. Our parents were in constant movement, separating, reattaching themselves to each other in a vagabond existence, their entrances and exits sudden and dramatic.

In Pozzecco, when my great-aunts unlocked the unused wing, I entered an alien space, cool and dank, my fantasy inverted. In the kitchen, dusty pots and pans hung against the wall; a 1950s dinette set with mildewed cushions stood in one corner, and in the living room, a faded couch and a grand piano. "It's just as your father left it," my grand-aunt said, as if he'd stepped out yesterday, and not three decades before. When I touched the keyboard cover, the left front leg of the piano pulverized in a cloud of sawdust. Termites eating through wood, time through memory.

Upstairs, in the bedroom wing, the long hallway was in shadow, punctuated at regular intervals by shafts of streetlight cast through seven windows opposite seven doors. On the walls inside each bedroom, the seven unmarried sisters, who lived out their lives in this house, stared back at me, their eyes piercing and accusing.

In Myanmar, too, three decades later, the dead stare out of frames. What do they think of all that's happened here, their glorious days forgotten, the green walls, stained and cracked, floor planks scratched and grey?

In the kitchen, mother and daughter squat on cut sheets of green linoleum around an iron pan, in which they've built a fire they feed with kindling. On top of this bubbles a pot of noodles. It looks so odd, as if they were squatters in this grand house, instead of the descendants of those faces in the photographs.

We thank them for letting us into their home and continue along the dusty road, past large, rolled-up coco mats, a cart and two white, humped cows, a motorcycle and a horse. We tie bandanas across our faces, like outlaws, to keep out the dust. Soon we cross Singu Creek, a dry tidal creek that resembles a vast riverbed. And on the other side, as we near Chauk, a petroleum port for the Singu-Chauk oil fields, oil derricks rise and fall like prehistoric animals feeding on the fragile ecology.

When we stop at the Chauk market, Lwin Thant explains that during the colonial period of 1855 to 1948, British Oil began using modern technology,

Morning arrival at Chauk market, Chauk, Magway Division, Myanmar

whereas previously, crude oil had been hauled out by bucket. Yet even that primitive method had generated immense fortunes for families. In 1902, he says, derricks were built and Chauk — once a desolate place of gullies and cliffs — was born. Forty years later, over 800 wells were producing 40,000 gallons of oil per day, until World War II, when many were destroyed.

I look around for riches and oil barons among the horse-and-buggies, the primitive wood fires, the market, where people stare at us as if we were strange creatures. Stalls overflow with yellow woven baskets of tomatoes, oranges, cabbages, purple aubergines, parsley, ginger; hands of bananas suspended from bamboo poles, rows of coconuts hanging in coco baskets; swirls of tie-dyed cloths; a woman seated on a red plastic pail, her child beside her, both of their faces white with thanakha. Everything so vivid, so vibrant, in contrast to the dismal statistics of the area — the lack of drinking water, the contaminated ground. It brings to mind Auden's comment on suffering in Bruegel's painting, *Landscape With the Fall of Icarus*: "… how it takes place / while someone else is eating or opening a window or just walking dully along…" While Icarus falls from the sky, in the foreground, people go about their business, ships sail calmly on and "everything turns away / quite leisurely from disaster…" Is this what we're doing, as well, turning away from strife and disaster within this country, eyes open, within our own country and cities and towns and villages and families, protagonists of our own stories, unaware of or indifferent to the suffering of others?

Past Chauk and the market, as we approach the bridge over the mighty Ayeyarwady River, Ileana says, "When we cross that bridge, it'll be new territory for us too." In the seven years she and Peter have lived in Myanmar, they have explored the country on many of their school breaks. Ileana's enthusiasm for a new experience mirrors my own.

"Let's cast off what we don't need," Frank says, "and begin new on the other side."

I think about what I could jettison for the rest of the trip. "I abandon all technology," I say, although this is unnecessary, because without a satellite phone and a suitcase of batteries, we would not be able to operate any tech devices. "And all that goes with it," I add, imagining email, YouTube videos and Facebook "friends" swirling in the river below.

"I will leave behind my negativity," Ileana says, surprising and delighting me, because Ileana has always been the pessimist to my Pollyanna. When asked how she is, or how an event was, she will most likely answer in the negative, "Not bad." I tend to seek out the positive, sometimes overcompensating — "It may have rained for a month, but the plants are happy!" — when Ileana's view is probably more realistic.

"I'll throw in any expectations I might have," Frank says.

"Easy for you," I say, because Frank approaches things without expectations.

"All right. I'll throw in my swimming trunks," he adds, and we all laugh nervously, thinking of the cold up ahead.

On this side of the river, as we progress towards the Chin Hills, we leave behind any fear of military personnel or informants; we are on our own. In Kazuma Village, we pass several trucks and oxen carts loaded with bamboo and wood bound for Chauk. At the side of the road, we stop to watch a family make thatch: expertly splitting bamboo into thin slats with machetes — no protective gear, no margin for error. Mother, father, daughter, son-in-law and granddaughter all work together, though the three younger ones stop

Woman making thatch from bamboo, Kazuma Village, Chin State, Myanmar

when we arrive. A ginger dog greets us, tail wagging. Lwin Thant speaks to the family in Burmese.

They all wear *longyis* and shirts and sweaters. The father's shirt, with cuffs carefully buttoned, is white and tucked into a green patterned *longyi*. The mother's *longyi* is black and over it she wears two sweaters—a light blue sweater over a brown one. Wrapped around her head is a red-and-blue scarf, made of thick woven cotton. We've seen many different ethnic groups with these colourful headdresses, each slightly different in colour and in design.

A rooster crows.

"Bah!" says the mother, and I hear *Chinbo,* among other words. She gestures with her machete to something in the distance.

"They are Chin," Lwin Thant explains, "but not from the mountains, and so they don't have tattoo on the face."

"Is she speaking in Chin or Burmese?" Frank asks.

Lwin Thant addresses the woman, who responds without looking up. "She speak both languages," Lwin Thant says, "but she is speaking Burmese."

"Look!" Peter says, "a Crested Serpent Eagle." We all turn to where he's pointing, but see nothing among the thick foliage. He hands the binoculars around, and we all peer, while he writes in his birding book. He is an avid birder, always on the lookout.

The family watches us watching the bird.

A rooster crows, loud and insistent. The woman continues to split bamboo, her voice rising and falling. I wonder how much narrative we're missing.

"They are farmers," Lwin Thant says, "and have a field over there." He points to the other side of the road. "But they make their money from thatch."

"If we'd met her in the jungle," the daughter says to Lwin Thant, studying me for a moment, "we would have all been scared of her and would have run away, because she is so white." We laugh, though it surprises me that they may never have encountered Western foreigners.

The Chin Hills, where we're headed—part of the Arkan mountain range that arcs for 965 kilometres between Myanmar and the Indian subcontinent—form a southward extension of the Himalayas into South-East Asia from neighbouring Manipur in India. We begin a steady uphill climb—the jeeps rattling and shaking—on sharp switchbacks, a cliff plunging beside us, the road a dusty stone washboard, intersected by creeks and rivers, washed-out bridges, or haphazard ones made of loosely spaced bamboo poles. We are all strangely silent, as if the bandanas have rendered us mute. We slowly manoeuvre past two ancient trucks loaded with ironwood that is secured precariously by a loose chain, and a logging truck sideways across the road. When we come to another, whose curved log makes it near impossible for us to pass, we scramble out of the jeeps and leave only the drivers to inch past the truck. We hold our breaths as the wheels come perilously close to the edge of the cliff, and I recall the long scar on my father's leg, another fragment of my parents' mythical lives, a romantic story of a party at the top of a Tuscan hill-town, and my father shuttling guests one by one on his motorcycle, in the dark, my mother out of reach, at the top or the bottom, when the wheels slipped, my father elusive, somewhere between intent and destination.

In mid-afternoon, we cross a small river to a clearing, where hundreds of bleached teak and ironwood logs lie stacked in mud, an old tractor rusting beside them. The late afternoon sun turns mud and water into a gold lagoon. In the distance, in what appears like slow motion, two carts loaded with bamboo and pulled by water buffalo approach and skirt by us, the large hand-made wooden wheels hugging the edges of the riverbed. I wonder if hidden among the bamboo poles is a valued teak or ironwood log going to market.

"This land, this wood, and this machine is owned by the government," Lwin Thant says. "The hardwood is cut in Chin state, near Kanpetlet. They have twenty elephants and they pull the logs from the jungle to the road. Machines put them onto trucks and bring them to this place. Then the merchants come and buy them." From here, the logs are trucked to New Bagan, loaded into ships and transported to Mandalay or Yangon. In Myanmar, teak, acacia, bamboo, and ironwood are raised and harvested for export, Myanmar being the leading supplier of teak in the international market. I imagine the extensive manpower, the time and effort involved, as well as the increasing deforestation caused by our voracious appetite for exotic hardwoods. In Yangon, Ileana has had custom furniture made from reclaimed teak. When we sit at her table, at her desk, when we open wardrobes and drawers, we can almost smell the salty air, feel the lurching sailing ships, hear an echo of the ocean a century away.

We proceed, climbing and climbing blue mountains. Below, fields sway in twilight, bamboo thickets surround us, the road switching back and forth. Up ahead, at the edge of a far cliff, the thatch roofs of Kanpetlet perch like grey market umbrellas. We stop at the only checkpoint we've encountered, and Lwin Thant presents our passports, permissions, and copies of our passports and permissions before we can proceed.

In darkness, we arrive at the lodge in Kanpetlet, the temperature near freezing. We layer on shirts, sweaters, and down jackets, then go to the main bungalow for a meal prepared by Maung Maung, a sweet young man who speaks a little English. We are the only guests here, shivering through rice and vegetables, clutching cups of green tea. We discuss a recent WikiLeaks from the US embassy in Yangon, stating that in the months following the devastation wreaked by cyclone Nargis, Burmese junta leader Than Shwe was considering a takeover bid for the Manchester United Football Club as a means of distracting the population from ongoing political and economic problems. We discuss the recent visit of American diplomat Joseph Yun, whose comments, after speaking to Daw Aung San Suu Kyi, were not very promising, and here considered disrespectful. We don't actually say the words *Aung San Suu Kyi*; we say *The Lady*. And I recall those days in Italy, when I was cautioned to ask no questions of my father's whereabouts, my mother's absence. My father, whose photographs show him in London, whose anti-fascist activities made him vulnerable in post-war Italy, a decade after the war. I wonder how long it will be before true democracy exists here, before there are no checkpoints, no fear of speaking a name; how long before there is more than a shellacked surface to lure investors and further fatten the wallets of those in power.

"There are many things people don't know," Lwin Thant says, lowering his voice, though there is no one else here. "There was an assassination attempt on *The Lady*, but at the last moment—"

The two drivers sit up straight, and speak to Lwin Thant in Burmese, their voices alarmed.

Lwin Thant stops talking, surprised, then waves them away. "They say, what if you are informers?" he tells us, and we all shake our heads and smile, but that's the end of the story.

In the morning, when we go to the main building for breakfast of scrambled eggs and coffee, the frost is evaporating from the thatched roofs. Huge gorges fall beside us, and up above, a mist across the bluish haze of peaks

Nat Ma Taung (also known as Mount Victoria) Chin State, Myanmar

creates an exotic, ethereal postcard of a mysterious land. *Utopia*. Ileana's painting *Migration*, in sepia and grey, layers a piece of Fra Carnevale's *The Ideal City*—a Renaissance vision of a better world—with disparate images "to create a hyper-reality, so that not only the conscious but the subconscious comes out too," she says. On top of the city, a guitar's strings are railway tracks moving into the distance; birds, normally a symbol of freedom, here are imprisoned by clouds; and in the right-hand corner, a person in silhouette stares across the water, as if there were another, better ideal city elsewhere.

"In that series," Ileana says, "I was examining identity and the loss of it when we move country to country." She pauses. "Although the immigrant moves towards the fantasy of a better life—the space of desire—the loss of identity causes new problems. I used these images because I wanted to layer the displaced person's memory, dreams, reality, disappointments." She stares out the window at the misty air, the circle of light at the crest of mountains. "But really, we are all displaced," she says, "either by war, emigration, jobs, death, desires. And once we leave home, we can never return to it as it was."

I wonder what she will call the paintings that will map this journey, with the two of us displaced and happy in this space of desire, this dystopian *Utopia*.

We linger, hands around the cups of hot instant coffee, until 7:00 a.m., when we set off for Nat Ma Taung or Mount Victoria, as the British renamed it, the highest mountain in Chin State and the second highest in Myanmar, on a very primitive road made of crushed rocks. We have seen how these roads are made—on other trips, we've come across young women at roadsides, hammering large stones into small chunks. As we drive, we pass a boy at the side of the road huddled in front of a small fire, then a barefoot young woman, who stops and stares at us with open mouth, both from villages one or two days away, on the other side of Mount Victoria. They walk to Kanpetlet to get various supplies, sleeping in the open at night.

We drive up and up—on my side, a deep canyon. I close my eyes now and then, the road so narrow I'm certain we're poised to plunge into the void below.

"Don't worry," Frank says, when he sees me leaning my body inwards, as if to steer the jeep away from the edge. "Soe Myint is a great driver."

"Let's sing," Ileana says, and begins "Chi Gettó La Luna New Rio," an Italian song, "Who Threw the Moon in the River?"

"To give me such sorrow," I sing, "Who threw it?" We have a repertoire of Italian songs our father taught us, and a series of other tunes we've picked up along the years, songs that require two-part harmonies. As children, we sang across Italian landscapes, then Canadian ones, and now as adults, we

Villagers carrying provisions up Nat Ma Taung to their village several days away

continue in Myanmar, Thailand, Cambodia. I would like us to create song-lines across the globe.

This stretch of road is only sixteen kilometres, yet it takes us over an hour to arrive at Base Camp. We are at 2700 metres, or approximately 8000 feet. We get out of the vehicles, and from the front jeep comes Maung Maung, now doubling as a guide to the top of Mount Victoria. We are in the midst of a subtropical moist broadleaf forest, between Kanpetlet to the south and Mindat to the north. Nat Ma Taung National Park is home to rare species of flowers, native orchids, and 200 species of birds. Peter is ready with his book and binoculars, eager to spot the rare White-browed Nuthatch, endemic to this area.

At the base, six villagers — four women and two men — are readying for their journey to the other side of the mountain. They are loaded down with supplies packed in large wicker baskets tied to headbands, the women in *longyis* and sweaters, blankets in vibrant magenta-and-blue checks around their shoulders, scarves wrapped across their mouths, the men in cargo pants and hoodies. All wear socks and flip-flops on their feet. We begin together, this seven-kilometre walk up to 3,200 metres, but they are soon out of sight. I wonder what they think of us, how privileged we must seem, in our fleece and running shoes, nothing on our backs. An hour into our walk, three young men pass us, carrying a large, heavy generator tied between two poles. They are fit and nimble, going up and down the mountain, through jungle, in their flip-flops and thin clothing.

TRACKS

Maung Maung leads us through a coniferous forest whose pines are covered in a grey moss used for medicinal purposes, past pearly everlasting, wild strawberry plants — not yet in season, large fragrant lavender trees, bamboo shrubs — valued for hedges. Lianas weave tree to tree; orchids spill from tree knuckles. Bird sounds are like water trickling. We're moving slowly now, unaccustomed to the steep grade. Ileana has wandered off, and we glimpse her now and then, when the path switches back or climbs steeply ahead of us. Frank and I walk with Maung Maung, who describes the medicinal properties of various plants. Now and then, he stoops, picks a branch of this or that, and puts it into his backpack. We've lost Peter altogether, but we think he must have returned to a lower elevation, because apparently, that's where the birds are.

"I have not travelled far from here," Maung Maung tells us, when we ask him where he's from. "Only to Mrauk U," in nearby Rakhine state.

"We've been there," I say, recalling Koe-thaung Temple, filled with 90,000 Buddha images. "The temples are incredible. And the scale…"

"Do you notice that the temples are in the shape of breasts?" Maung Maung asks.

I laugh. "I thought they were in the shape of helmets," I say. "Like monuments to some war."

Maung Maung laughs with us. "No, no. There is a legend," he says, then goes on to describe a love story between a queen and a mason, a jealous king, a glimpse of a naked breast, and of course, the death of the star-crossed lovers. I write it all down in my journal.

When we round a corner, Ileana is standing at a V in the path. "I wasn't sure which way to go," she says.

Maung Maung leads the way, and I fall into step with Ileana. A half hour earlier, she tells me, she came across seven villagers seated at the side of the path. They offered her an orange out of their packs, even though they'd walked for days to buy their supplies. She shook her head, but they would not take no for an answer. One of them spoke a little English, and asked where she was from.

"Canada," she said, "but I live in Yangon." She had no idea whether they knew what or where Canada was. "And where is your village?" she asked them.

"Seven mountain ranges," the young man said, pointing into the distance. "We walk four days to Kanpetlet."

"So," I say, "when you're here, you say Canada is home. Is Canada home?" She shrugs.

We walk in silence for a few minutes. At 3000 metres, we are in a high montane forest of lush oaks and rhododendrons, and on the ground, small bluebells.

BURMESE GOTHIC

"I was thinking," Ileana says, "about that painting *Origins*."

It's one of my favourites of the series and depicts the skeleton of death as a new beginning; two cows dying of drought, like immigrants who are not nourished in the new place; three trees, their roots visible on the surface, reach to the depths of the earth; and viewed from the back are Ileana, my mother and me, squatting in a semi-circle, staring at something unseen on the ground.

"Mom, in her old-fashioned dress, represents the past; the semi-naked me in a bikini is between the two worlds, while you are fully dressed in pants and T-shirt."

"I didn't feel so wholly formed, nor so adjusted," I say. "Not at that age."

"Nevertheless," she says.

At the side of the path, frost begins to appear here and there. Then, a wicked wind picks up, and we scramble for our jackets. Up ahead, another steep slope to climb. However, the top of the mountain is now in view, or at least a promising expanse of blue. Then, a spectacular panorama unfolds, a Chinese painting—nine layers of mountains and valleys silkscreened against the sky; Bangladesh, India in the distance; thick thick jungle, tall tall bamboo below us, and clinging to the edge of the abyss, trees gnarled and shaped by wind into intricate silhouettes. It is a breathtaking moment, a sudden awareness, a freedom from everything we strive for back home. My imagined utopia is almost palpable, just out of reach, a receding horizon, spurring me on, inviting belief in magic, in the spiritual world so evident to the people, in the Nats so present everywhere.

Mixed media painting, Origins, *by Ileana Springer*

THE UNFORESEEABLE FUTURE

We begin our three-hour trip to Mindat in late afternoon, travelling too quickly on a washboard road. Terraced fields sway brown and dusty in the valleys; indigo mountains rise around us. As twilight descends, the road stops at the edge of a river and an arrow points us onto another road, muddy, wet, through another village, down into more mud, through water, and I realize we are now on a riverbed. For a moment, a fear flutters in my stomach. I think of all those stories of tourists being detoured to their certain deaths. We are back to trust, that "tentative and intrinsically fragile response to our ignorance." I take a deep breath. Isn't this exactly what I was looking for?

My fear dissipates in the eerie dusk, in the flames of small wood fires along the detour route. The bridge looms over us — one span missing. The driver starts to cross the riverbed, but the water is too deep and he abandons the attempt. Darkness has fallen quickly, as it does in the jungle. Further along the bank, we can see a makeshift bridge: a few logs across the span, with a series of thin bamboo poles laid crossways to create a surface to drive on. We stop and wait as the open jeep makes the precarious crossing. The bamboo poles clatter and bounce under the jeep's wheels. We follow, then drive in darkness for what seems like an eternity, until we arrive at the Mountain Oasis Resort — a series of spartan bungalows similar to those in Kanpetlet — though a little more primitive, due, perhaps, to the lower temperature, the lack of common area or restaurant.

Htaik, a Chin interpreter, emerges from the shadows. He is tall and thin, and wears jeans and a thin, grey windbreaker. I wonder how long he's been waiting. Among the foliage, to one side of the bungalows, two boys stoke a fire beneath a large metal drum.

"They are making hot water," Lwin Thant says. "You can have shower."

The temperature has dropped considerably, and the thought of removing my clothes and getting wet sends shivers up my spine. We all take quick sponge baths, then climb back into the jeeps and head to a restaurant ten minutes away, where we eat supper, coats on, feet frozen. Then we are back at the bungalows, and Frank and I huddle in a single bed, fully clothed, covers over our heads.

In the morning, we drive to Mindat, the capital of Southern Chin State, and stop at a small restaurant perched on the edge of a cliff, overlooking the valley below. If we were to lean out the window, we'd see the building's stilt supports reaching to a landing far below. This is typical of Chin housing — the front along the edge of the mountain, the back supported by towering stilts that, as legend goes, were meant as safety from tigers, leopards and other wild creatures. The practice continues, although through poaching and the destruction of habitats, tigers and leopards are rare. I suspect the heavy rains and steep valleys may have more to do with why houses are built at the top of the mountain, on the crests of cliffs.

A man enters and sits down at the next table. He's in western clothing and doesn't look like the others here; perhaps his stare is too intense, his stance too assured and inquisitive. He is watching us. I glance at Ileana and can see that she is aware of him too. The man makes a great show of pushing back his chair, stands up and holds out his hand to us, which we each, in turn, take and shake.

"Good morning," he says, scrutinizing us.

I am certain he is military, and am immediately nervous, even though I haven't done anything to be nervous about. It's like going through a US

Woman with Müün clan tattoo

border these days; there's a certain amount of paranoia and fear, even when one is innocent.

"Where do you come from?" he asks.

"Canada," we say.

"Canada," he repeats. He sits back down, but faces us rather than his table. "How long will you be staying?"

It feels like a test we might fail. For a crazy moment, I imagine myself telling him that we're here to help Mrs. Mang Dang, daughter of a Burmese woman and a British commanding officer during WWII, who has been labelled an illegal foreigner and expelled by the military because of her British heritage.

"We're just travelling through," Peter says. "Lovely country."

A boy approaches with a thermos of hot water and cups with packages of instant cappuccino resting in the saucers.

The man does not have a friendly face, and when he smiles, his eyes narrow. He switches to Burmese and speaks to Lwin Thant, who responds in clipped sentences. I wonder what he is asking about us. I stare down at my cup, busy myself ripping open the instant coffee package and pouring in hot water.

As quickly as he appeared, the man leaves. Lwin Thant smiles and we all smile back. I wonder if Lwin Thant is an informer.

This area of southern Chin State, Htaik tells us, called by its people K'cho land, is particularly distinctive because it is one of the last places in Myanmar where women's faces are tattooed. Two years ago, when we went to Mrauk U, south and east of here, in Rakhine State, we took a boat upriver to Pan Paung, a village where lived the "last five Chin tattooed women," our guide told us then. While they were the last five women with facial tattoos in that village, in southern Chin state, where we are now, the practice has continued, especially in the more remote villages, despite the fact that facial tattooing has been outlawed since the 1960s. In the townships, we are told, the practice stopped in the 1980s, but we see women in their twenties with facial tattoos.

According to legend, facial tattooing began in the eleventh century, when kings and ruling princes would scour the countryside and take the most beautiful women for slaves or concubines. The tattooing was meant as a disfigurement, thereby not only saving the women from capture, but also helping to identify those who were captured. Somewhere between the eleventh century and now, tattoos became a symbol of strength, good luck and beauty. In K'cho, the facial tattoo is called "Mang Gruke": "mang" meaning good luck or wealth; "gruke" meaning to adorn and beautify. The tattooing ink is made from pinewood soot mixed with various leaves such as

Headman and wife, Mindat, Chin State, Myanmar

lobster-bean leaf paste, that when pressed, turns into a green liquid. Thorns are used to puncture the skin.

"They are for politeness and beauty," Htaik says. "It is like a man standing without clothes. When he is dressed, he is more polite."

After breakfast, our drivers go in search of other drivers for news and road conditions, while we climb a small wooden ladder from the street to the property of a man who used to be the headman in his village, and wait with Lwin Thant and the interpreter in a verdant garden. The headman's village is about thirty kilometres from here, but the family now lives in Mindat.

Before the British annexation of the late 1880s, K'Cho headmen governed over villages, their positions inherited. They had total power as decision-makers, judges, and religious leaders. "Nowadays, however," the headman says when he joins us, "in the townships, the government has taken over, so the headman's job is finished." He sighs. "In the village," he says, "if someone divorces or fights, the headman can take care of all that. Even if someone murders someone. As long as they go to the headman, they don't have to go to town."

Everything in this country is a contradiction. I have read that headmen in northeast Chin state are government-appointed thugs who regularly extort money from villagers. And as peaceful as all appears to be here right now, according to Chin Human Rights Organization (CHRO) up north, where we are not allowed to go, villagers are routinely subjected to forced labour by the military, to act as porters or work on the construction of fences and military housing, which makes it difficult for villagers to farm and work for their own families. Often entire villages are "fined" sums of money for invented infractions — and this of the people who, according to a UN statement, live in the poorest state in Myanmar.

The headman holds a long handmade rifle and points to the stump where his hand should be. "I did this by myself, in accident," he says. He wears a headdress — red turban, white band and black knot in front, in which are imbedded two bamboo sticks decorated with nine or ten white rooster feathers, creating two elaborate bird tails. Across his chest lies a conch of gunpowder, and a wide black strap as armour against knife wounds. He became headman in 1960, when he was eighteen, he tells us, having inherited the position from his grandfather, who was given the headmanship by the British. Although he encourages us to photograph him, he never looks at the camera. I later discover that in Myanmar, direct eye contact is perceived as an act of challenge. In fact, our guide tells us, men who know each other well don't make eye contact with men, so as not to appear distrustful, nor with women, so as not to appear sexually aggressive.

The people of Mindat and Kanpetlet are of three ethnic groups, the Müün, the Dai, and the M'Kaang. Here in Mindat, they speak K'Cho, a language that was purely an oral language until 1924, when an American missionary, the Reverend Cope, began to establish a written system, decided it was impossible, and gave up. However, a few years later, in 1932, Colonel Burne, Falam District Magistrate, asked Cope to try again to establish a written language. A committee was assembled, a writing system established, and textbooks printed so that in 1933, 1935 and 1936, the K'Cho language was taught in schools.

During WWII, all K'Cho language schools were closed and students sent to Buddhist monasteries. For thirty years, the language was not taught, although there were two attempts at reviving it, the second of which produced a beginner's textbook in 1976. The teaching of the K'Cho language began anew. Because the same textbook was used for all levels of teaching, in 1977 a new committee was established to create appropriate textbooks for all grades. The textbooks were typeset and ready to go to press, but were never printed, and the teaching of K'Cho language disappeared for another decade.

In 1986, a new committee revised the K'Cho system of written language, but the 1988 political unrest effectively ended this endeavour. There have been no K'Cho language classes since then. Young people are memorizing oral history in songs from their grandparents, although they do not understand some of the old vocabulary no longer in use.

THE UNFORESEEABLE FUTURE

The headman's wife's face is thick with M'Kaang clan dot tattoos — the spots of a leopard — made when she was twenty. I try to imagine what she would have endured. The pain must have been excruciating, and she would have known she could die if the wounds became infected. She would have borne it bravely, though, because tattooed women are considered the strongest, and most desirable, and are assured the best husbands. Around her neck hang two dozen strings of beads — yellow, blue, green, black, white. Silver belts encircle her waist, and in her earlobes — which are gigantic and reach almost to her shoulders — are two huge hollow gourds, intricately decorated with yellow, red, blue and white beads. "These earrings are for celebrations," she tells us. The daily ones are three-inch pieces of bamboo, which, traditionally, would have held a roll of money. Her hair is parted in the middle, swept up at the back, and held in place with a deer-shin hairpin.

She holds a bamboo flute, which is played with the nose — a custom particular to this area. Traditionally, a marriage proposal and acceptance were expressed through the playing of this flute. She begins to play, but she has a cold, and can only make several strange sounds. She shakes her head and passes the flute to the headman, who plays a haunting melody, after which they invite us upstairs into their home, which consists of one large room where all family interaction occurs. This house has more furniture than we've seen elsewhere: against one wall, three dressers full of books, papers, and blankets; against another, a couple of chairs and a coffee table. On top of the dressers are hats, a wind-up clock, a plastic radio, an old boom box, and various containers. On the wall above these hang framed graduation pictures of their children. Pinned to the other wall are calendars and family photographs. Curtains partition sleeping areas. We sit on coco mats, careful not to show the soles of our feet, nor to point them at anyone. On the floor lies an empty liquor bottle, a cane, and a beautiful old teak trunk, out of which spills the arm of a blue sweater.

"I had ten girlfriends," the headman says, his eyes twinkling.

"I have thirty!" his son says. They all laugh, appreciatively.

The women do not seem perturbed by these confessions.

The interpreter explains that with power, the men get women.

I wonder what happens to the women, and ask, "What happens if an unmarried woman sleeps with a man?"

"She must marry him," the headman says. "And if she sleeps with a man who leaves her, then she is considered married, and no one in the village will marry her."

I imagine forty single women living alone somewhere in the village.

"However," the headman adds, "if a man sleeps with a married woman, he can be killed by the family of the husband."

We leave the couple's house and continue down a treacherous road along the edge of the cliff to our last destination for today — the fortune-teller's house. On the way, we stop to look at memorial stones, which resemble large stone tables — under which are laid the ashes of the family, under the male lineage.

"The village comes to honour the dead," Lwin Thant says, "and the family kills a mithan to feed them all. It is very costly. But then, they earn the stone."

We climb back into the jeeps, and Ileana says, "Do you remember when Zio Gaetano died?"

"Sort of," I say. Zio Gaetano was my surrogate father, a kind and humorous man, who died in his early forties, when I was six.

"When Zio Gaetano died," Ileana says, "no one told me. I was happily playing in the garden, when Grandpa came out said, 'How *could you* be playing outside, when your uncle has just died upstairs?' How was I to know if no one had told me? I felt mortified. It was so *unfair*."

She's right. Back then, no one spoke to children about important things. We had to discover everything through other means. And later, Ileana tells me, she was not allowed to go to the funeral, "as if I were not part of the family," she says. She was sent to school, and left to wonder about the flowers and black cars, the coffin and the cemetery, where she sneaked to after school, terrified that she would be caught. "It was my first death," she says.

What I recall are my uncle's white face and hands, the cool marble skin, the absolute stillness of his body laid out in the living room, and my aunt lying tragically across her bed, ice packs on her forehead. I don't recall a funeral, nor do I recall Ileana being there.

"When I would visit you," Ileana says, "if anything bad happened, I was always blamed for it." She pauses. "You could do no wrong."

"That doesn't mean I had it easy," I say.

When in Rutigliano, Ileana was *other*, in my space. While I was a chameleon who could change colour depending on whom I was with, Ileana wore her rage up front, hands clenched and ready to strike.

When I went to Udine, I was *other*, timid in Ileana's tangled outdoor garden. She woke me out of afternoon naps, coaxed me into dark sheds, climbed up and down broadleaved trees, while I hovered in a dainty, smocked dress, in awe and fear and wonder.

"None of it was easy," she says, then we arrive at the fortune-teller's house, climb down a steep set of stairs sculpted in the cliff, past two children, to the bottom, where a young woman weaves brilliant purple cotton. She has extensive Müün-clan facial tattoos: the fan of a peacock's plumage on her forehead, tiger whiskers below her nose and on her cheeks, horizontal lines decorated with half-moons.

THE UNFORESEEABLE FUTURE

Her husband waves us into his fortune-telling lair, a separate thatched hut, in the corner of which is a bricked-in fireplace and a still of what is probably K'cho Yu, a traditional drink brewed from red millet. I think about the great possibility of fire — given the woven bamboo walls and coco mats. The fortune-teller welcomes us into the windowless room and motions us to sit on the floor. Directly across from this hut is another thatched hut, "For Buddhist prayer," he tells us.

While 90% of Burmese follow Theravada Buddhism, in practice, popular Burmese Buddhism coexists with astrology, numerology, fortune-telling, and the veneration of Nats. During our various trips to Myanmar, we've heard apocryphal tales stemming from the generals' devotion to astrologers and fortune-tellers. For example, on our first trip here in 2006, we inquired about the small sickly castor plants that languished in front of every house. The official story is that the government, intent on producing biofuel, had ordered everyone in the country, on threat of fines or imprisonment, to plant the castor plants, even in desert areas where drinking water was scarce, despite the incredible hardship this caused the people. To this day, no castor plant has been harvested. Later, however, we heard a much more interesting story: apparently, the name of Aung Sang Suu Kyi and the name of the castor plant (Kyet Su) are exact opposites — that is, the two names reversed: Suu Kyi and Kyet Su. The generals, being superstitious, followed their astrologers' and fortune-tellers' advice that by planting the Kyet Su all over Myanmar, they would be bringing bad luck to Aung Sang Suu Kyi. As well, people were instructed to plant the castor plant *outside* their properties — something the generals believed would make *The Lady* leave the country and stay out. Astrologers are so revered that the military junta relocated the capital city of Myanmar on one's warning that a foreign attack on Yangon was imminent. The move to the newly created city of Naypyidaw began on November 6, 2005, at the astrologically auspicious time of 6:37 a.m.

Here in Chin State, the K'Cho Chin believe nature has a direct connection to spirits who can help solve the problems of daily lives — how to secure food, prevent or cure illness, avoid dangers. Fortune tellers are consulted for anything from business to travel to "violence clearing," meaning any kind of bad luck. "We don't believe in psychiatrist," Htaik tells us. "If people have trouble, they visit the fortune-tellers to find a solution." The K'Cho make offerings to appease both white and black spirits, with many sacrifices necessary to keep the black spirits at bay. All this sounds remarkably like animism with a dash of Christianity. In fact, a large percentage of the Chin population was converted to Christianity by British and American missionaries at the turn of the century. The current government has launched an attack against them by supporting Buddhist schools only, and forcing Christians to pay high fees to send their children to school. The result is that many Christians declare themselves Buddhists so that their children can get an education.

Before we begin, the fortune-teller assures us that he has a personal connection to the spirits, that he is, essentially, the spiritual guru of Chin State. He is the fortune-teller. He is the Buddhist. He believes in the Nats, the spirits. I try to reconcile the animism, Buddhism, and occultism. Here, it appears, past, present and future co-exist without conflict. Multiple indemnity—nod to every possible higher power, and your good afterlife chances increase. I marvel at the very idea of a seer; who wouldn't want a glimpse of the future? I immediately volunteer to go first.

The fortune-teller draws an egg out of a basket, hands it to me, and asks me what I want to know. "What's in my future?" I say vaguely, not wanting to reveal any information he could use.

He takes the egg, and with a small piece of bone, taps a hole at either end, then blows into one until all the yolk and albumen ooze out. I study the liquid mass carefully, imagining what he might read into this. Instead, he draws out a dagger and carefully scores the eggshell.

At his call, a young boy takes embers out of the fireplace and places them in a bowl. The fortune-teller inserts the bone in the fire and, when the end

Fortune-teller of the unforeseeable future

glows red, he rubs it against the eggshell, slowly and methodically, creating an ashen backdrop, exposing black sword ridges. Then with a piece of moss, he scours the entire shell. I am fascinated by his amazing crooked index finger, like the one witches in fairy tales have.

Ten minutes or more have passed when he looks up and asks, "When you left your home, was it raining or dry?"

Vancouver in December. I say, "Raining."

"Aha!" he says. "I see a rain symbol on the egg." Then he begins rubbing the burning bone over it again, as if to make a rain pattern on the eggshell.

A small chick wanders into the room, its downy feathers askew. It hops around, oblivious to us. In one quick swoop of the arm, the fortune-teller swipes the chick off the floor and out the door. He doesn't even look up.

Then he turns to Htaik and me. "I see good economics," he says. *Good economics*, yes: we are in remote Chin State, with a guide, a Chin interpreter, two jeeps and two drivers.

"On the day you left your home, one of your children had a headache or maybe a head injury," the fortune-teller says, looking at me expectantly.

I am silent for a moment — not for dramatic effect, but because I don't know how to say this without embarrassing him in front of Htaik. Finally, I say, "I don't have any children."

He looks surprised, puzzled, but he recovers quickly, and says, "One of your siblings then, your brother or your sister."

I say, "Well, both my brother and my sister live very far away from me, so I don't know if they had a headache or head injury." Again, he looks puzzled. How strange we must seem to him, no children, our family thousands of kilometres apart, and we think nothing of it.

Ileana, who so far has been sitting very quietly, now sweetly says, "Maybe I had a headache last Monday."

She is trying to help this fortune-teller. I want to help him too. "Could it be my mother?" I ask. "I think she had a headache."

He sighs, then goes back to his burning bone. I try to find something else to ask him, something simple. In a few days, we'll be trekking in Shan state and we have been told it'll be very cold at night, so I ask him, "Will we be very cold on the next trip?"

He relaxes visibly. "It's going to be cold, but don't be afraid. At night, if it's cold, you need to wear a hat to keep warm." He sets the bone to one side of the bowl, but it falls over. The burning end flickers and sets the coco mat on fire — a small flame, yes, but one that has Frank, Ileana and me all apprehensive, in this windowless room, a still of alcohol beside us, and the only door on the other side of the fire. All three of us stare intently at the small flame on the coco mat, willing it to go out. At the last possible moment, the fortune-teller reaches over and slaps the fire out with his open palm. He puts the bone back in the bowl, picks up the moss, rubs it over the egg once more, then hands it to me, saying I must break it into two pieces, and when I get outside, I must throw one in front of me and one behind me. I follow his instructions in the sunshine, after giving him a suitable amount of money for the fortune un-telling.

In late afternoon, back at the lodge, Ileana and I walk up the road. The sun is low in the sky, and the air brisk. Men, women and children — some as young as three — emerge from the jungle and woods in a slow procession up the hill towards town, carrying firewood in preparation for the evening cold. Some are barefoot. None have appropriate warm clothing. Later on, they will huddle around small fires beside their huts. As we walk, Ileana and I reminisce about those summers in Pozzecco, where we played outdoors, wild and unmonitored, running through fields of corn, just the two of us, not yet imagining ourselves on different continents, driving down mountains on potholed one-lane roads, over rickety bridges, across rivers whose currents are dammed by sticks and stones, through banana plantations, coconut, palms, and fields and fields, in love with people, jungle, trees, huts, goats, dogs, oxen.

An old truck drives about a metre past us, then stops. Two men get out. I catch my breath, thinking of this lonely road, the two of us defenceless. The men reach into the back of the truck and pull out a tray of sweets — sticky rice around palm candy, rolled in coconut shreds — and hold them out to us. This moment, this offering, this brief connection, is the photograph not taken, the indelible memory: two men in twilight, the moon rising against an indigo sky, a horizon of peaks.

EXCAVATIONS

*All water has a perfect memory and is forever trying
to get back to where it was.*

— Toni Morrison

CROSTOLI, INTRIGONI, BUGIE

The aroma of deep-fried delicacies wafts from the open window of my mother's kitchen, releases memories of *home*. It's July 1992, and my aunt Ninetta's arrival from Verona has precipitated a family reunion, albeit a small one, as my mother, uncle, nephew and I form a tiny splinter group in Vancouver. Inside, my mother and aunt are laughing; I rap on the kitchen window to get their attention, while *La Traviata* blisters from the speakers in the living room.

This is Zia Ninetta's first trip to Canada, and my mother is anxious to repay the hospitality she enjoyed when she visited my aunt in Italy. In the past month, she has painted the guest room, sewn a new bedspread and cushion covers, driven to Bosa on Victoria Avenue to buy *taralli*, Italian olives, *panettone*, figs, mascarpone, mozzarella, and enough flour to bake for eternity. This, from my artist mother, who although uninterested in cooking when we were small, as the years pass, experiments endlessly to rediscover recipes her mother made, resulting in strange, savoury delicacies, vaguely familiar, as if in our collective memory there exists a familial palate.

Married to brothers, my mother and Zia Ninetta spent their twenties and early thirties in Trieste and Udine together, their history intertwined. They were accomplices against my grandparents, who had hoped my father would marry someone "more suited to him," meaning a fellow student he had met in Tuscany when he was sixteen, and with whom his sister had developed a friendship, although my father had not encouraged the relationship, nor corresponded with the young woman in the intervening years. I suspect my grandparents objected to my mother's crimson lips, her outspoken disposition, and her larger-than-life personality. In Zia Ninetta, my mother found a kindred soul, a free spirit from Verona who loved fashion and parties. They formed an allegiance.

My memories of Zia Ninetta are forged from black-and-white photographs in family albums. Within the white deckled edges of the small snapshots, Zia Ninetta smiles into the camera, her arm around my mother, and beside them, my father and uncle, looking handsome and dangerous. They all resembled movie stars — the men with glistening hair, white shirts and dark sunglasses, the two women in stylish sweaters, midi-skirts and platform shoes in front of the Uffizi Gallery in Florence, in striped bathing suits in Rimini, in sundresses and sunhats in outdoor cafés in Venice — celebrities in my eyes, the women carefree and casually bold, decades before the women's movements of the 60s and 70s.

This is the mother I never knew, the mother I imagined as a gypsy, freed from the manacles of culture, of her parents' disapproval. A gypsy with golden bangles, tiered skirts and anklets, whose small brass bells announced her presence. A gypsy, and not my widow mother, who awoke alone to a frigid Canadian morning in 1972, my father in a morgue downtown.

How different our lives turn out, despite all we envision, our vision marred by the unexpected — a speeding car, an undelivered letter, a heart attack in the afternoon.

Today, Ninetta is the widow who greets me at the door. She is a formidable presence, a handsome woman, with large blue eyes and hair combed into a bun. She wears a turquoise shirtdress and a string of translucent pearls. We embrace, then she holds me at arm's length, trying to recognize me, though she hasn't seen me since I was a toddler. "You look like your father," she says, fingers on my cheek. "The Donati fair, fair skin."

"Come in, come in," my mother says, clearly relieved, pulling me into the kitchen. Always glamorous, she is impeccably dressed in a white silk shirt tucked into natural linen pants, her chestnut hair cascading in soft waves around her face. "We're going to make *crostoli*."

Her voice lilts in lively, spirited tones, fuelled, I'm certain, by competition. Because they originate from different regions in Italy, my mother and Zia Ninetta make different *crostoli*, and my mother will manage to turn the baking into a competition, and her version of *crostoli* the best.

Like most national delicacies, *crostoli* change name and recipe by region or town, as if to embody the personalities of its inhabitants. In Genova, Torino and Imperia, they are called *bugie* — lies; in Toscana, they are *crogetti*, or *cenci* — rags; in Sulmona and centro Abruzzo, they are *cioffe*; in Sicilia, Campania, Lazio, Sardegna, Umbria, Puglia, Calabria, and Milano they are *chiacchiere* — gossip; in Reggio Emilia they become *intrigoni* — intrigues; while in Parma, Modena, Bologna, and Romagna they are *sfrappole*, or *rosoni* — rosettes. The names of these delicacies are as numerous as the towns and people who make them, supplementing and altering the recipes to suit their tastes: *galàni, sfrappe, sprelle, lasagne, lattughe, pampuglie, stracci, manzole, fiocchetti,* and so on. Interesting to note that while some of the Italian names are flippant — "lies, intrigues, gossip" — the English name for these is an earnest "angel wings," the cannibalistic suggestion notwithstanding.

"*Vieni, vieni,*" Zia Ninetta says, her hand on my elbow, leading me into the kitchen. "We're just setting up."

I breathe in, imagining the fragrance of dough deep-frying in our first Canadian home in Kitimat, where a week before Christmas, my mother would cover the kitchen counters, dining room table, and two card tables with clean tablecloths and a variety of small implements: a fluted pastry wheel, a knife, a small bowl of water, as well as several large platters, neatly stacked. My father would reach into the uppermost shelves of the pantry and retrieve the pasta machine in its original packaging. Despite the box's curled and droopy edges, the machine inside was like a shiny new car, chrome-plated and heavy with our memories. My father would secure the machine to the edge of the counter with a C-clamp, then slide the handle into its slot. We all washed our hands, pushed up the sleeves of our sweaters, tied on aprons, and began our yearly ritual — in this, we were always united.

The opera crescendos at the party scene where Alfredo sings *Libiamo, Libiamo,* the famous drinking song. As soon as Violetta begins her part — *Tra voi / tra voi saprò dividere / il tempo mio giocondo* — my mother, Zia Ninetta and I spontaneously begin to sing along, gesticulating as if we were welcoming guests to a nineteenth-century ball, our hands flitting imaginary fans in front of our faces — *Tutto è follia nel mondo / Ciò che non è piacer. All in the world is folly / if it is not pleasure.* My mother has a rich soprano, while Zia Ninetta's voice is husky — a sound I associate with Friulan, the language of Friuli — its warm contralto a memory of my father, who taught us Friulan songs with the most unlikely romantic plots — a moon/love thrown into the river and retrieved by a net of stars/kisses. In music, too, we were always united.

"Actually," Zia Ninetta says, when we've stopped whirling about and are back to opening bags of flour and unfolding tablecloths and dish towels, "at home, we only make *crostoli* during Carnival."

In Italy, these treats are most commonly made and eaten during the fourteen days before Lent, when, in the Christian tradition, fasting and sacrifice begins and extends for forty days, until Easter. Carnival — the feast before the famine — originates from the Latin *carne* (meat) *-levare* (lift), meaning to remove meat from one's diet. So this season is a *hello* to sweets and partying, immediately preceding *farewell* to meat.

"Well, we don't believe in all that nonsense," my mother says. "Those old men starving themselves and beating themselves with ropes... " She shakes her head. "We make *crostoli* whenever we have a festive occasion."

Verbena as a young painter in Bari, Italy

Though isolated from the rest of the family in Italy, we observe our own rituals and traditions, albeit either modified to suit us or invented here. For example, our birthdays are not complete without a St. Honoré cake from Fratelli Bakery on Commercial Drive, a family reunion definitely requires rice croquettes and *panzerotti*, Christmas would not be Christmas without *crostoli*, and my mother would not be my mother if she couldn't revise traditions at will.

"And today is definitely a festive occasion, Zia, because you're here with us," I say quickly, hoping to discourage a religious tangent of conversation focussing on fasting and self-denial, two things I am not interested in.

For the next half hour, we set our *crostoli* stage. Everything we touch turns into narrative: kitchen counters, tablecloths, utensils, water, even the opera — and soon we are deep in memory, recounting stories, as if this act of cooking together has forged a passage to the past. Our small disclosures bridge years and countries and disparate lives.

When everything is ready, we begin.

This is how we make *crostoli*: empty onto a counter a large amount of flour mixed with nutmeg and cinnamon; excavate a hole in the centre, creating a lovely white spent volcano. Heat olive oil together with the peel of a lemon. When the peel sizzles, strain it out, and pour the hot oil into the centre of the volcano (which now sputters and spits like a live volcano). Add water to make a manageable dough.

"What are you doing?" Zia Ninetta says, frowning while my mother builds her small white mountain.

CROSTOLI, INTRIGONI, BUGIE

My mother turns, eyebrows raised. "What do you think?"

The small ensuing pause swells with Violetta's and Alfredo's farewell duet. I sigh, and swallow. I can't listen to *La Traviata* without weeping.

"What about the eggs?" Zia Ninetta says.

"We don't put eggs in *crostoli*," my mother says, dismissing her.

Zia Ninetta frowns at me. I shrug. All I have is my mother's word for how to make these delicacies. And she, I assume, has her mother's word. Mirrors facing each other, extending to infinity. I retrieve a small pot from the cupboard and pour in olive oil. Then I draw a lemon out of the fridge and cut off large chunks of peel, which I drop into the oil.

"You're not going to use oil?" Zia Ninetta says, alarmed.

"Of course we are," my mother says briskly. "What else would we use?"

I slide the pot on the stove and turn up the gas.

"Butter," Zia Ninetta says. "They're made with butter." She eyes the tables. "And where is the grappa?"

"Grappa?" My mother looks at her watch.

"For the dough," Ninetta says, hand wiping imaginary dust off the counter. "But a glass of wine would be quite welcome later on." She pauses, staring out the window at the flowering mock orange to one side of the deck. From the living room come the plaintive arias of Violetta, who, pressured by Alfredo's father, has agreed to forsake Alfredo and now makes Germont swear that she will not be forgotten. *Dite alla giovine / si bella e pura...* "Don't you remember those good times we had in Udine?" Zia Ninetta laughs a throaty, ironic laugh.

My mother turns. "You always got away with murder."

A subtle shift, and we slide into dangerous territory, into the remnants of a feud begun years ago: an insinuation that money from my father's Italian bank account was used to bail out Zio Danilo's foolish spending, without my parents' knowledge. It's one of those topics no one has ever broached straight on, but rather that we all agree to pretend we simultaneously know and don't know the details. What is certain is that it caused bad blood between my father and his brother. And when my grandfather died, my father and Zio Danilo inherited two houses in Udine, joined by a porte-cochère, which perfectly symbolized their relationship: linked yet separate.

"That's not fair," Zia Ninetta says. "I didn't do anything."

"No, you didn't have to. You were born in the right family. An only child."

I continue to stir the oil, listening to *La Traviata*, an opera so familiar, I can recite every line. Violetta Valéry, born into the wrong family, destined to remain a courtesan or ruin a man's reputation. The power of tradition, of prejudice. *Addio, del passato / bei sogni rident / le rose del volto / già son pallenti...*

"I had nothing to do with that," Zia Ninetta says.

"My family was made poor by the war and the sanctions, but we were proud," my mother says, and recounts how she designed and sewed exquisite outfits from blankets and curtains, à la Scarlett O'Hara, outfits that looked expensive. For this, she was chastised by her mother-in-law, who was convinced my mother would ruin her son. "I was the bad one in her eyes," my mother says, "while you were beautifully decked out in furs and dresses Danilo bought quite likely with—"

Zia Ninetta draws in her breath. "I know nothing about that," she says. "You know I don't." Her mouth is set tight.

My mother turns back to her flour, and Zia Ninetta continues to wipe a small area of the counter. "How could you *not* know?" my mother says. "Did you not speak to your husband?"

I stare from one to the other — these beautiful, self-possessed women — trying to imagine them in Italy, contrasting and exotic, friends and competitors for my grandparents' love.

Love is the heartbeat of the entire universe / mysterious
mysterious lordly / cross / cross delight / cross and delight / to the heart

"Our husbands were the ones who got away with murder," Zia Ninetta says. "They were charming womanizers."

We are all silent now, while Violetta and Alfredo declare their undying love for each other, their intention to leave Paris and live happily ever after in unmarried bliss, a plot turn that requires a suspension of disbelief, given the era of the opera and the obvious consumption of the heroine. My mother sifts flour through white fingers; Zia Ninetta riffles through her purse for a tissue.

"We'd better get working," I say, "or the *crostoli* won't be ready for supper." I pause. "Seeing as you make them in different ways, why don't we try both recipes?"

"We don't have grappa in the house."

"It doesn't have to be grappa," Zia Ninetta says. "Spirits. Surely you have some of those?"

My mother frowns at Zia Ninetta, trying to decide if this is a dig or not. "We have wine," she says, "and anisette, amaretto and Grand Marnier."

"Any of those will do," Zia Ninetta says, "but the anisette would be best, because it's colourless." She rolls up the sleeves of her dress, and ties on the apron my mother offers. Then she washes her hands, and gathers the flour bag.

The competition begins.

CROSTOLI, INTRIGONI, BUGIE

Zia Ninetta spills flour into a bowl, cuts in the butter, beats the eggs in a second bowl, then adds all the ingredients but the icing sugar. She folds the dry ingredients into the wet ones until she has a ball of dough, which she encases in plastic wrap and puts in the fridge. "There," she says. "Now we have to wait a couple of hours for the liqueur to ferment into the dough." She opens the door, lets in a lozenge of sun. A warm breeze filters in.

My mother raises her eyebrows. "You're joking."

Zia Ninetta shrugs. "That's what my mother always did," she says. "I think it has something to do with the pastry puffing up better." She unties her apron, slips it off, then wipes her brow with it.

On the deck, a cluster of fig trees form a seductive oasis of shade, an escape.

"Our *crostoli* always puff," my mother says, "and we don't lay the dough to rest."

"No, we don't like laying things to rest," I say.

My mother laughs. She is a veritable dynamo, both vivacious and tempestuous.

"All right." Zia Ninetta's voice is both resigned and frustrated. She dons the apron and slides the dough out of the fridge. "Let's just make them now."

Both of them knead and roll their dough into logs, slice off two-inch pieces they first flatten with a rolling pin, then hand me to pass through the rollers of the pasta machine. The thinner the dough, the greater the puff.

Zia Ninetta places her pastry sheets on her side of the kitchen, and using the fluted pastry wheel, cuts rectangles, in the centre of which she makes two cuts.

My mother abides by our tradition and wheels the pastry cutter along the length of her pastry sheets, creating bows, diamonds, and rosettes shaped from long strips of dough, pinched at one-inch intervals, then spiralled together.

"Listen," Zia Ninetta says, "I almost hate to mention it, but I think what you're making is not *crostoli* but *cartellate*."

My mother looks at her, amused. "Call them whatever you like," she says. "In our family, we have always called them *crostoli*."

We continue to roll and cut, until every surface in the kitchen and dining room is covered in various fragile shapes, some of which do resemble angel wings. Now comes the deep-frying, a delicate, messy job.

My mother reaches into the pantry and extracts the *crostoli*-frying pot — the bottom of an old pressure cooker we owned in the early 70s that my mother has carted house to house ever since. I haul out the tin of olive oil.

"That pot is much too deep," Zia Ninetta says, peering into its depths. "Don't you have a frying pan? Really, you only need an inch or so of oil."

"Oh no, no," my mother says, "*crostoli* are deep-fried. You can't deep-fry in an inch of oil."

"Well, we never deep-fry ours," Zia Ninetta says. "They would become too greasy."

"It's the exact opposite!" my mother cries. "When you drop dough into deep hot oil, it sears the outside, and doesn't allow any oil inside." She pauses. "When you fry them in a shallow pan, they absorb the oil."

"Let's eat them raw," I say.

They both turn to me, and I grin. "Just kidding. Seeing as we're making two batches," I say, "why not use two different pans?" And I bend down and pull out my mother's frying pan for Zia Ninetta.

They shrug, and fill their crucibles with oil. When the kitchen turns cobalt with smoke, they drop handfuls of *crostoli* into the pots, turn them over, and whisk them into the colanders beside them, all in less than a minute. Then they wait for the oil to blue-smoke again. I transfer the drained *crostoli* onto large platters.

"These look just the same to me," I say, holding the two platters side by side.

We all stare at the golden, puffed *crostoli*.

"Close your eyes, both of you," I say. "Let's see if you can tell one from the other."

They close their eyes. I make a lot of noise to confuse them, then I give my mother one of hers, and Zia Ninetta one of hers. They each correctly identify it as their own recipes. "Wait, wait," I say. "Let me give you the other one before you decide." And then I give them each one of their own again.

"The second one is definitely Ninetta's," my mother says. "The eggs give it a slightly different consistency."

"I think now the first one is definitely Verbena's," Zia Ninetta says. "A little crunchier."

"You are both absolutely right," I say, tasting one of each myself. "And both are delicious."

A plume of blue air swirls past us. My mother smiles and takes Zia Ninetta's arm. "Let's finish so we can pour that glass of wine," she says.

We proceed to the last step, where the two versions diverge. Zia Ninetta dusts her batch with icing sugar, while my mother pours a tub of honey, a couple of spoons of sugar, a little water and a handful of pine nuts into a pot on the stove. When the honey bubbles up the sides of the pot, she submerges the *crostoli*, a few at a time, then quickly drops them into the platter I hold beneath her hand to catch gleaming, steaming, sticky delicacies, pine nuts — like memories — embedded in their hollows.

CROSTOLI, INTRIGONI, BUGIE

We now have two platters of *crostoli*, both different and similar. My mother and Zia Ninetta exchange recipes. I inhale deeply—a sensory inheritance—the fragrance of our early days here, and I think of the last vestiges of our family in Canada—two nieces, a nephew—who have never made *crostoli* in a hot kitchen with my mother, blue smoke swirling and dissipating in the air.

My Mother's Crostoli Recipe

Flour
Nutmeg and cinnamon
Salt
Olive oil
The peel of a lemon
Water to make a manageable dough
Honey
Sugar—small amount in the honey
Pine nuts

Zia Ninetta's Crostoli Recipe

6 eggs
6 tsps of sugar
6 tsps of crumbled butter
6 tsps of vanilla extract
1 envelope of icing sugar
1 heaping tbsp of salt
1 glass of grappa or liqueur (light, or else the dough will be dark), or if you have good wine, put ¾ of liqueur and ¼ wine

Use as much flour as you would when making pasta

TRACKS — MAY 2006

I'm in a rented car, at a railway crossing on the outskirts of Rutigliano, in southern Italy, when the train passes and the squeal of its wheels on metal transports me to a time before my birth, to a 1940 night sky in Locorotondo, where from her room my aunt Ida watched trains emerge and disappear into the railroad cutting in front of my grandparents' house.

It's May 2006, and I've spent the last month at the bedside of this aunt who, over the past five years, has told me her life story so often, I have begun to appropriate it, weeping and laughing in all the right places, mouthing the words right along with her. Ida is the guardian of our family stories, our oral historian. She claims absolute knowledge of everyone — despite my mother's objections — and will recite particulars from all our lives, in dramatic arcs, complete with dialogue — mythologies which are difficult to prove or disprove.

I have been taking daily drives into the countryside to escape the weight of her past which, for the most part, Ida recounts in tragic, melodramatic tones, ending in maudlin, self-pitying sentences such as, *Oh, how I've suffered!* and *I have worn out my threshold of pain.* During these afternoon drives, I can breathe deeply, unencumbered by her reproach, which feels directed at me even though her stories occurred decades before my birth.

I cross the tracks, and continue along the highway. On either side, rows upon rows of vines spread their arms beneath the mammoth nets that protect the grapes from hail, like prisoners praying for rescue, their legs tied, their heads back, faces to the merciless sun. As I drive on, the sky darkens with thunderclouds, and a surge of excitement — a memory — presses against my temples. I follow it to Locorotondo, tracing the map in my aunt's head, the map of a young girl walking to school in the morning snow, flanked by her two brothers, Pippi and Alberto, all of them in paper-thin shoes and rough hand-knitted sweaters, all of them happy, carefree, Ida tells me, in a way she's never felt since.

I approach the town from the north, drive up into it, up up past the school where Ida spent that year teaching small children, past the overlook at the park where old men on benches gaze at the sprawling valley below.

My grandparents moved here in July of 1940, a month after Mussolini declared war on the Allied Forces. As a trackman, and also because of his difficult nature, *Nonno* had been relocated so often his seven children — of whom Ida was the eldest — were dizzy with disruptions, unable to make friends and wary of strangers, who constituted everyone outside the family. It explains, perhaps, Ida's melancholy, her persistent memory, although she attributes it to Fridays — the day of her birth — which she tells me is unlucky, because it's the day Christ died. *A day of superstitions*, she says, a small ironic smile curling her lips. Back then, people did not shop on Fridays or begin new projects or sign contracts or plan feasts. On Fridays, she tells me, people did not marry, nor did they baptize their children. If a man shaved on a Friday, he would be betrayed by his wife, or he would become widowed at an early age, and he who cut his nails on this day would have to gather them on Judgement Day. One did not go visiting, send gifts, nor buy clothes, and if the first day of the year was a Friday, there would be wars, tempests and a thousand other natural disasters. Furthermore, she tells me triumphantly, children born on Fridays can expect to cry often during their lives — and this Ida has proven to be true.

My grandparents' *Casello Ferrovia #72* — the trackman's hut — is situated next to a railway crossing, the tracks of which wind below the hill, two kilometres from Locorotondo, in the Valle d'Itria, which is not actually a valley but a karstic depression, a firmament of green hills and vales studded with over 20,000 *trulli* — the white conical ancient dwellings — and

Hillside town: Locorotondo, Italy

with limestone farmhouses. Locorotondo — round place, as the name suggests — is one of numerous stupendous towns found throughout southern Italy, built on hilltops and fortified by immense walls and towers. Inside are medieval cities, all remarkably preserved. From the highways at night, these towns look magical, lit up like multiple nativity scenes.

Locorotondo rises 1400 metres above sea level, one of three natural balconies that surround the valley, and from which one can admire the Mediterranean brush, an indigenous vegetation that includes groves of Macedonian, bay and holm oak, laurel, myrtle, hawthorn, lentisk, wild olives and black orchids. Nowadays, this valley is dominated by vineyards and country estates, a patchwork of red earth handkerchiefs stitched together by stone walls. When my grandparents lived there all those years ago, however, they knew nothing of castles or monuments, didn't realize the oaks were 800 years old. All they saw was a pervading green, stone walls built without mortar, fields of red poppies and yellow daisies. And at night, outside their window, the town appeared suspended in darkness.

It takes several tries before I can decipher how to reach the *casello*. I have to return to the lookout, to fix my memory — my aunt's memory — on the green on green, forget the new developments, the villas, and the asphalt roads which slice through the valley, and concentrate on the wild brush, the faint chugging of a steam engine in my head. Eventually, I spy a dirt trail that circles to the right, and following it, soon find myself in Ida's youth, surrounded by small limestone walls covered in lichen, fields of forage swaying, and bunches of red poppies growing amongst the rock. I follow the railway tracks directly to their *casello* on the half-metre path beside the tracks, around the circular waist-high wall to the front. On these paths, *Nonno* rode his bicycle to work, and each morning, the children walked to the station more than a kilometre away, to catch the train for school. On this path, in the cutting which rises high above my head, my aunt learned about the earth, about rocks, stratification, about fossils visible in the limestone. They seemed wider back then, she tells me later, welcoming, these paths which led them into the world outside the family, paths which in memory have expanded both in size and significance.

The *casello* itself is changed and yet the same. One of the windows has been bricked in, and against the wooden door is a padlocked steel grate. At the back, the oven gapes like a yawn in the afternoon sun. I lean my head in and close my eyes, breathing in the distant scent of *Nonna's* bread on Mondays, imagining the children's mouths watering. They were allowed only one slice a day, "until the war ends," *Nonno* said, and the children dreamt of loaves of bread. They had so little, even their dreams were small. *It seemed a marvellous childhood, Ida tells me. We were dying of hunger, we*

Casello No. 72 – trackman house of Genni's grandparents

had fleas so large we had to smash them with hammers, we had mosquitoes that ate us raw, and yet everything felt normal at the time. We had bread, and a house to live in, and we were very fortunate. As well, because we didn't know anyone who was wealthy, we had no comparisons to make. Not like now, with TV, where everyone knows how the wealthy of the world live.

I walk around the small circular yard surrounded by stone, where for one summer, *Nonno* grew tomatoes, zucchini, aubergines, potatoes and onions, where Ida planted geraniums between the rocks. None of this is evident now, the gardens reclaimed by nature's wild grasses and flowers. Everything has been dwarfed by age, but I have only to close my eyes, and the *casello* is vivid with their nine lives, with their perfect happiness constructed inside my head.

Across the tracks from the *casello*, a small road leads up and over a rise. I follow it, past the abandoned *trulli*, where decades ago lived a young woman who grew red roses, flowers my aunt had never seen before, past a *carrozzeria* — a fairly recent car graveyard surrounded by a chain-link fence — past wild trees of cherry, almond, fig and hazelnut, past the sprawling sculptures of flowering cactuses, imagining the taste of *fichi d'India* — prickly pears — of my own youth, past swishing *biada* and golden lichen on the white white walls, heading for the end of the road, toward a story my aunt has told and retold so often that I feel as if I, too, am part of that

November evening in 1940, after supper, when *Nonno* and *Nonna* heard the sound of thunder in the distance. *Nonna* crossed herself and cast a worried look toward the smallest child, Alberto, who sat at the table drawing. He had been born during a thunderstorm, and she believed that babies born during thunderstorms have a lifelong tendency to tremble, that they fear things will collapse on them, that their sparkling eyes cannot hold another's gaze, that they have brilliant ideas and thoughts but cannot articulate them because they will always be thinking about thunder and the possibility of the earth breaking open and swallowing them whole.

The thunder continued, but sounded strange—at times like a punctuation, other times drawn out. "It's a bombing," *Nonno* said suddenly. "Get the boys up."

Nonna and Ida quickly awakened all the children and together they ran to the top of the hill, from which they could see the lights of the port of Taranto on the Adriatic coast, with its arsenal and shipyards, chemical works, iron and steel foundries and food-processing factories. In the darkness, the thirty kilometres of verdant fields in front of them disappeared. Mario, who read the newspapers every day, told them that the entire Italian fleet was harboured there, and that Taranto was impenetrable, with its shoreline cannons and its metal nets under water, so that even submarines could not reach the ships.

But even as he said this, airplanes swirled in the sky like a flock of pelicans over a school of fish and dropped hundreds of torpedoes and flares into the harbour. The Italian cannons fired back non-stop. Projectiles flew hundreds of metres into the air. The sky was ablaze, the air thick with thunderclaps. Every now and then, a deafening blast echoed underfoot, the sky brightened into an artificial dawn and they knew a ship had exploded. In that 1940 darkness, those spectacular, recurring bombings seemed like fireworks. The boys hollered and sprang in the air, feverish with excitement, arms out, fists punching the sky; fortunately, they were too young to join the army, but they were childish enough to be fascinated by the idea of war. This, despite the fact that since the war had begun, *Nonno* had been listing the horrors, using his and his brothers' experiences in WWI as examples—a completely unsuccessful tactic, given that unfazed, the boys continued to construct guns and cannons from which they launched pieces of wood and pine cones against imaginary foes, which often included their siblings.

In the following day's newspaper, they read, "Last night, a large number of British enemy torpedoes attacked the port of Taranto, extensively damaging numerous ships of our military fleet." They were stunned. Hadn't they been told Taranto was impenetrable? Wasn't Italy going to become a superpower?

Of course, they didn't realize what the state-controlled papers did not say: that all the ships had been sunk.

My aunt went outside and crossed the tracks to the little country chapel across from the *casello*, opened the gate and knelt in front of the Madonna and Child frescoed onto the back wall. She understood nothing of politics — it seems impossible now to think that while atrocities proliferated around them, the family existed in a pocket of staggering ignorance. Ida says they were so poor and so hungry, for them the war was a phenomenon occurring in a distant parallel universe that had nothing to do with their inside world of babies and children, where the dangers far outweighed any external imminent one — Pippi could step on a rusty nail; Alberto could drink stagnant water and contract typhoid; Bruno could succumb to pneumonia; Bianca could slide under the wheels of a train. They were constantly vigilant. Living, itself, was a danger.

In that little chapel, my aunt prayed for everyone: for all the sailors who surely had been killed, for all their wives and children, for the British soldiers who had dropped the bombs, for their wives and children who would have to live with the knowledge of these deaths, for her siblings who seemed unbearably vulnerable, and for her mother and father who, she suddenly understood, couldn't protect them from unspeakable evil.

I leave the hilltop and walk back to the *casello*, past the country chapel that, with the exception of a locked iron gate, has remained exactly as my aunt described it, back towards my air-conditioned car, imagining the sound of thunder, thinking how fortunate we are to never have witnessed war in our comfortable houses in Canada, to never have had to cower in our beds, expecting the sound of sirens.

I hear a train and quickly move off the tracks, experiencing a small moment of fear, like Ida must have — worried about the children, overly sensitive, overly morbid, always searching for the dark side of things.

The train is a pathetic old thing, four wagons only, all dirty and graffitied. I watch it turn the bend in the cutting, thinking how unlike what my aunt remembers, this decrepit train hobbling along, anachronistic in the wealthy landscape, the villas and superhighways nearby. I think how sad *Nonno* would have felt to see it, for surely it would have diminished him to witness its uselessness. And I think of my aunt, and for a moment, I feel the depth of her sorrow, her premonition that everything is gone, and that her awareness sprung of that night in 1940 was merely the beginning of a long line of disillusionments that would populate the rest of her life.

TRACKS — OCTOBER 2007

I used to stand at railway tracks, my toes against the ties, while trains approached. I held my breath as they lumbered past, tuned to the whine of metal on metal, their weight a tornado in my chest, their speed reverberating in my heart.

"You are crazy," my brother told me years later. "Don't you realize how lucky you are that you weren't decapitated?"

He should know, transportation safety being his line of work. He pointed out the obvious dangers: 1) the air turbulence around the train; 2) the stabilizing 6x6 stakes in the side pockets of the rail car that can fly out; and 3) the banding straps holding the loads in place that can come undone at one end and become gigantic moving razorblades, band-saws, guillotines.

I pondered the possibilities of these unpleasant dangers, recalling a railway track in White Rock where I once saw a decapitated cat — head on the ties, body on the gravel, neatly severed, as if the cat had chosen that exact moment to cross.

"And not only that," my brother continued, "do you know the anxiety you're causing the conductors on board?" He paused. "When they see someone that close to the tracks, they assume it's a suicide waiting to happen. Can you imagine watching that and being able to do nothing about it?"

Late afternoon in Roma Termini, a torrent of travellers ripples to and fro — tourists, Italians commuting to jobs, families, businessmen/women. I move among them in trepidation of my return to Rutigliano, a place intrinsically tied to my childhood, with its joys and sorrows, a place I've returned to repeatedly in the past decade. I spent my early childhood here with my aunt Ida, who loved me so extravagantly, I sometimes worry she loves the little girl rather than the adult in front of her, her memory of me as intact as mine of her.

Zia Ida and Genni pose on the balcony, Rutigliano, Italy

At Binario 19, I board my train for this journey between Rome and Rutigliano, this familiar buffer between my Canadian city life and my aunt's inner life.

We glide slowly out of the city, the train almost soundless on its high-speed rail. Graffiti brands every available visible surface: trains, fences, the sides of ties, posts, the walls of buildings bordering the railyard — an urban clamour for attention. Trains skirt the rear of cities, the buildings blackened with soot, images you won't find in guidebooks of monuments and sculptures, of obelisks and paintings and seaside festivals. Trains traverse the landscape, anonymous and familiar, their whistles time signals, their coaches magic carpets to a better life, their weight an awakening vibration over ballast and ties, over the gravel and broken stone of lives.

In the past year and a half since my last visit to Zia Ida, I've remained steadfast in my belief that she is immutable, though my uncle has warned me that *she is changed.*

The Eurostar slowly picks up speed. There is no lulling sound to this train, no rhythmic clack-clack clack-clack, no side-to-side motion. We shoot past Roman walls, archways, ruins, a pine forest, yellow and red buildings, terracotta roofs, open fields, farms, olive groves, vineyards. We enter tunnel after tunnel, wide valleys, the Apennines in the distance, and finally the Mediterranean. I have taken this journey so often, I can almost close my eyes and still see ruins, tilled fields, cows, buildings, herds of sheep, all mixed together, old and new.

TRACKS

She is changed, my cousins say, without explanation, their tones apologetic, tender. I hear *changed for the better*, though my Zia Ida is etched inside me as perfect: one of the people on earth who has always loved me completely and unconditionally.

In twilight, stones begin to appear in the fields, more and more of them, then stone fences, stone terraces holding back hills, stone walls encased in chicken wire. Then fields of wild cacti, laden with prickly-pears. This is an arid area of Italy, and water for agriculture is brought here by the Apuglian Aqueduct, which stretches for over 2000 kilometres, and passes through 99 tunnels and over 91 bridges — an unbelievable feat, like love.

Near Bari, nostalgia settles in my chest, not for myself, but for my mother, who lived here until she was thirty. I wish she was with me to recount her stories, her past elusive. Buildings assume the verdigris of clouds reflected in the dusk. I long, too, for the Zia Ida of memory, anxious about the changes. When I called her from Rome, her voice was languorous, detached. I think of all the times I didn't phone her, because she'd want to talk for hours and hours, lamenting, always lamenting. Zia Ida has always seen the glass half-empty, as if she is incapable of joy.

Swarms of birds fly low; tall tall pines sway like black umbrellas against the darkling sky. At the station in Bari, I settle on a circular stone bench outside, under a yellow light, waiting for my cousin Maria-Antonietta. Beyond the station platform rises an island of palms and eucalypti. A man crosses the tracks and sits facing me, eyeing me openly, in the way some men do in these southern cities. I pull my bag next to my body. He slides across the bench, closer, and I slide an equidistance away. I cross my arms and stare straight ahead. Undaunted, he moves closer, as if my being alone in early evening is an invitation. It reminds me of another time, another journey, a departure from Bari at night.

I was travelling to Udine, in northern Italy, to visit one of my cousins. When the overnight train arrived, I asked if I could upgrade my seat to a couchette. The conductor shook his head. The night train was booked solid, he said. I begged him to check for a cancellation. He shook his head again, said he'd see, and boarded the sleeping car. I waited, undeterred, until presently, he returned to say that yes, indeed, he had had a cancellation, and I could have the couchette. I thanked him and settled in.

A half-hour into the journey, when I was already in pajamas, a knock startled me. I opened the door slightly, and found the conductor holding not a ticket punch, but a bottle, which he held out.

"I thought you might like some champagne," he said.

For a stupid moment, I stared at him, uncomprehending. Then, I realized what was being asked, and was furious that he could be so presumptuous.

I gritted my teeth, said a polite, "No, thank you," and shut the door and locked it, even though I was uncomfortably aware that he probably had a key.

Later, when I retold this story, I wanted to change the ending: "I took the champagne bottle, said 'thank you' and shut the door in his face" or "I slapped him and shut the door in his face." That's what I should have done, though here in southern Italy, in the 1980s, men still considered foreign women or women from northern Italy — identifiable as I am by my fair skin and red hair — to be *fair* game. This attitude towards women came to international attention in 1999, when in a rape case, an Italian judge ruled that a young woman couldn't have been raped because she was wearing jeans, which could not be removed without her help. The next day, three female members of parliament wore jeans and lobbied against the judge, sarcastically proclaiming that now all women were safe, thanks to him, as long as they wore these "anti-rape" jeans. Of course, nothing came of this, and the rapist was set free. However, in 2008 when a man tried to use that earlier judgment to get an acquittal in a molestation case, he was found guilty by a court which ruled that "jeans cannot be compared to any type of chastity belt."

I like to believe attitudes towards women are changing, but now here in Bari, the man at the train station lights a cigarette and blows smoke towards me, as if we're in a steamy bar in a black-and-white movie. I want to roll my eyes at him, but I look away instead. Fortunately, my cousin arrives, and soon, we are headed for Rutigliano.

Elma, my aunt's housekeeper, is waiting at the open door. We hug happily. She is family now, has been with my aunt for ten years, since Zia Ida rescued her from an unscrupulous employer who — after bringing her on a government program from the Philippines — kept her in a tiny airless room, and forced her to clean his friends' houses on weekends. Zia Ida sponsored Elma's husband, Sammy, and their child Ian, who is now eleven. During the past decade, Elma has had two more children: Giulia, five, and about a year ago, Marco, who all consider Zia Ida their grandmother. They all live here with her, a three-generational family.

"You must not expect your aunt to be the same," Elma says to me. "She is okay, but not the same."

I walk down the hall to Zia Ida's room, my heels clicking on the marble tile. Last door on the left, and there she is, as always, in bed, and I rush to embrace her.

She looks up, languid, her eyes indifferent.

I draw in my breath, and lean down to kiss her cheek. She smiles weakly, and I try to hide my disappointment, hold her hand and say her name.

On other visits, my aunt's eyes would light up with utter joy on seeing me. Today, nothing. She lies there, passive, looking at me, but I could be anyone.

"Zia Ida is having a bad day today," Elma says, quietly, patting my back. "And it's late. Maybe tomorrow…"

A bad day, I repeat in my head, *a bad day*, as if the sun were responsible. Tomorrow she'll sit up, and we'll talk for hours. *A bad day*, a tape loop. The warnings return. *She is changed*, they all said. This is more than a change, this is a vacancy. I think of all the summers I've spent with her this past decade, grateful to have listened to her stories. Has she given up now that she's given me the saga of her life — the tracks she's followed and left behind? Isn't this what we all crave: to be remembered as we recall ourselves?

Zia Ida closes her eyes and falls asleep. Elma leads me out to the kitchen, where she makes me a cup of coffee, though in Italy no one drinks coffee at night. We speak easily, because Elma speaks perfect English as well as Italian and Tagalog.

"Probably a small stroke," Elma says. "Not enough to do too much damage, but some …"

"She is so passive," I say, a giant lump in my throat. "It doesn't seem like her at all."

"Today she is not having a good day," Elma repeats. "But you'll see, tomorrow or the next day, she'll be better."

How does one recuperate from a life gone wrong? All her friends are dead. She has few visitors, the family scattered around Italy, and us in Canada. My cousin thinks Zia Ida was in love with a married man, and when he died in 1998, she went to bed, relinquishing life. My mother thinks Zia Ida is lazy and instead of lying around, should have been doing something to make her life meaningful. I think there's truth to both. After all, being in love with a married man is a kind of laziness, and when Zia Ida took to her bed, I suspect she believed that like a tragic heroine of a nineteenth-century novel, she would die of a broken heart. Instead, here she is, almost ninety, and as my uncle says, "with the inner organs of a thirty-year-old. She'll outlive us all." For her, being alive is a suffering.

Elma has set up a cot for me in the living room for tonight. Tomorrow, I'll go to a hotel, though throughout my life and visits, I have always slept here, in my aunt's room, beside her, the two of us whispering all night.

I turn out the lights and lie on the cot, eyes closed. How different this time is from all the others before, now that my aunt is no longer herself. She is the one who recalls me as a child, the link to my childhood memories. How will I remember my small self as the years pass?

After a while, I open my eyes and am startled by an eerie oblong light shining in a corner of the ceiling. At first, I assume it's a reflection from the street below, inverted through the glass balcony doors, like a mirage. In childhood, I spent my days inside this house and played alone within a high-walled garden. At night, I lay in bed and invented stories of life on the street below to match the flickering shadows on the ceiling.

I look at the balcony doors, but the curtains are drawn. I close my eyes. It's my imagination, and I should not indulge it, but I have an uneasy feeling. In this room my ancestors have lived and died; their faces stare out of portraits on the walls. I wonder what they could tell me of my aunt and of myself, of everyone who has ever lived here. I wonder what lurks behind the austere gazes, and whether there was ever any joy. I am not superstitious, yet in this house, who can say what is or isn't? I wait a while, then open my eyes. The oblong light is still shining in the corner.

Perhaps my aunt has died in the other room, and this is her spirit come to see me, to talk to me. I stare at it, trying to discern something, but it's indiscernible. Finally, I whisper, "*Ma chi se tu?*" *But who are you?* Predictably, there's no response.

I close my eyes again, on the verge of believing in ghosts and spirits, in this lonely old house in southern Italy, where everything is possible. I get up, and slowly walk toward the light, hypnotized by the possibilities of the unknown. Directly below that eerie glow, I bow my head. My cell phone lies face-up on the floor, its oblong screen projected onto the ceiling.

In the morning, my cousin drives me to the only hotel in town. I sit on the single bed, in the small spartan room, dismayed by how quickly my expectations have been undermined, like karst topography, the cave-in on the inside. I want to return to my aunt's room, to her apartment, to the same old house where I spent my early childhood. I want to return to the same place, to the same memory. I want to return.

I don't unpack, but leave my suitcase on a chair and step outside. Pools of water polkadot the strips of sidewalk, which are, at most, a metre wide, and often not even that, so that I have to step onto a narrow medieval road barely wider than a car. I hop and sidestep puddles as I go. I don't recognize anything, the hotel in an area I don't normally frequent. I am a fifteen-minute walk from my aunt's house. Partway there, I realize I've forgotten a packet of photos, so I turn back to get them.

As I near a house, a woman emerges and stands in her doorway, hands on hips, watching me. The cliché of a southern Italian woman, she is small, squat, dressed completely in black, kerchief tied under her chin. She has a larger sidewalk in front of her house, colonized with two chairs and a small table. I skirt it, trying to avoid the large puddle on the road when she begins to shout at me. She's speaking in a dialect I don't understand. I have been raised to speak only Italian. However, the tone of her voice implies that she's angry, or perhaps, cursing me. I edge further away, gingerly stepping into the water on the street, while she continues to yell. Maybe, I think irrationally, she knows I was born in Trieste, and therefore, am from the North, which means that she *is* cursing me, and calling me who-knows-what names. I hurry past, head down, while she continues to hurl curses and damnations at me.

Once at the hotel, I pick up the photos, and head back.

I have barely come into view of her house when the woman emerges quickly, as if she has been waiting for me, and stands in her doorway, hands on hips, yelling. I am known here as *La Genni, La Canadese*, whose mother they all recall, and ask me about. I nod politely, tell them my mother is fine, yes, still painting. She has remained a young woman in their eyes, a thirty-year-old who escaped this town, whose adventures in another country they can only imagine.

The woman is still yelling, and this time, I decide to face her and smile, so as to disarm her and dissuade her from her cursing. I look up. She gesticulates madly, arms waving me closer to her house, and I realize that she has been trying to coax me onto her area, so as not to get my feet wet. What I perceived as cursing was a courteous invitation to avoid the water. I thank her, and walk on, thinking how easily one can misinterpret, without knowing. What else have I misinterpreted? Who else have I misjudged?

This I know: my aunt, a woman who has always been formidable, feared, who commanded attention, has had a stroke which has rendered her docile. It's disconcerting to sit at her bedside while she lies, silent, unless I speak to her. How unlike herself she is, the aunt who has lived through us all. How often I have lain in the dark of her bedroom, listening to her urgent outpouring, as if there were not enough time in our lives to say everything. Perhaps she was anticipating this exact moment, this path from which we can never return.

I spend the mornings with her, then walk around the countryside in the early afternoons, when she naps, and everyone is inside at *pranzo*. In less than a kilometre, I cross a bridge over a Roman aqueduct and find myself in olive groves and vineyards. I circle the town several times, burning away the anxiety I feel over this new aunt. Instead of she being the storyteller, our roles have reversed. I am now the one who speaks of my mother, of us all in Canada, of all the years I've been away. She listens intently, nods in all the right places, but when I finish whatever story, she asks me questions that confirm that she has not grasped what I've said. At the end of each day, I return to the hotel downhearted.

Some afternoons, I board a train and ride to nearby towns, where I wander, aimless, across cobblestone streets, around Roman walls, inside churches and outdoor markets. At dusk, I wait for the next train, my toes against the ties, my brother's words in my ears: *Can you imagine watching that and being able to do nothing about it?*

Two days before I'm to leave, Ian comes in from school, excited. "*Nonna, Nonna,*" he calls.

Zia Ida stirs. She loves Ian intensely; she loves all her adopted grandchildren. I know this from other visits. She pats the bed. "Come. Sit here."

"Today, we studied Dante!" he says, and from his school satchel takes out his scribbler.

"Bravo," she says.

"Dante was born in Florence in May or June 1265," Ian says, bouncing on the bed. "In 1285, he married Gemma Donati. That was your surname too, wasn't it, Zia Genni?"

I nod. "Before I got married," I say. We are descendants of that Florentine family.

"Before you got married three times," Zia Ida says.

I'm amazed that she remembers this, and wonder what would have happened had she remarried when she was left a widow. In this small town, it would have been almost impossible for her to have a second romance at the age of thirty-three, a woman who was barren. We have all deserted her, I think, to make our own lives, to escape her expectations.

"This is what we learned," Ian says, and begins to recite the beginning of the *Inferno*:

*Nel mezzo del cammin di nostra vita
mi ritrovai per una selva oscura,
ché la diritta via era smarrita.*

*Midway upon the journey of our life
I found myself within a shadowed forest,
for the path which led aright had disappeared.*

I am enchanted by his intensity and delight. He's in grade five. I can't imagine Canadian grade-school children citing Dante. I can't imagine Canadian university-educated adults citing Dante, unless they're pursuing a degree in literature or classics. In fact, last term, in my first-year university creative writing class, my students proudly announced they didn't read literature. This omission was reflected in their stories, which began innocently enough, that is to say, they began as stories about people like themselves or their parents, or their imagined versions of people older than themselves —wizened old men of thirty, forty-year-old grandmothers who thought only of knitting and baking, etc. However, once established — however thinly — these benign characters suddenly and inexplicably stabbed people on buses, shot everyone at work, quartered and ate children, dismembered friends over drug deals, and did so in agonizing detail, so that every single wound, every severed body part was lovingly described.

As I read from one story to the next, the pattern continued, and soon I felt as if I were watching TV, the channels switching so quickly it was impossible to catch the narratives or the motives — only a continual outpouring of blood — a violence as obscene as it was nonsensical and sensational.

These young people were not writing their own stories, but those reflected from television, their stories someone else's version of reality — a fictional world of crime and adventure, a cartoonish existence of surfaces.

Perhaps, I then thought, this is actually a reflection of our culture and society. Perhaps they really are mirroring their market-driven manufactured selves.

In contrast to this, here, in Italy, schoolchildren study Latin, Greek and philosophy in high school. What better way to understand the roots of words, the roots of logic and reason? Schoolchildren can name sculptors, poets, artists; they can recite classic poems, point to monuments and know who built them; recognize paintings and painters; they are proud of their heritage, and knowledgeable about history. I wonder why our education system has been dumbed down, as if we don't believe our children are capable of or interested in learning.

By the second line of Dante's *Inferno*, my aunt is reciting with him. She knows the entire poem by heart.

"That's as far as we got today," Ian says after another verse, and closes his scribbler.

"Go and get the big book," Zia Ida says.

Ian hops off the bed, goes to the den, and returns moments later with an illustrated version of *The Divine Comedy*, which he opens, lovingly, to the *Inferno* page, and continues to read. Zia Ida's eyes sparkle, and she intones the words aloud with him.

After a few verses, Ian closes the book, and says he has homework to do.

"Do you want me to keep reading?" I ask her.

"*Magari!*" she says. *I wish*!

I open the book, and begin to read, my tongue tripping on the archaic Italian. Zia Ida recites along with me, often correcting my pronunciation. Whatever memory she might have lost, this is not it.

TRACKS — OCTOBER 2007

I sit at her bedside all afternoon and read *The Divine Comedy*, which she knows by heart and follows intently, stopping me only to say, "You know what that means, don't you?" and to explain. Or she anticipates: "This is the part where they come to the burning lake."

I've stood at railway tracks, my toes against the ties, while trains approach. Now I sit at my aunt's bedside, my hand in hers, and hold my breath as years lumber past, tuned to the whine of flesh and bone. Today, we journey together through Dante's *Inferno*, through his *Purgatory* and *Paradise*, our eyes wet, our hearts open to each other, to the magic that is poetry — a language through which we can finally communicate.

DIS-LOCATION

You can never go home again, but the truth is
you can never leave home, so it's all right.

— Maya Angelou

"I'm on my way to the airport," my mother says one bright Saturday afternoon, "and I've already called a taxi."

"The airport?" I say, guarded. "Where are you going?"

"I'm going to Ottawa to buy a house," she says.

I don't miss a beat. "I can drive you," I say. "Why do you need a taxi?"

It's July 2011, and after forty years of living in Vancouver, my eighty-seven-year-old mother has decided to relocate in Ottawa, 4000 kilometres away. This is not the first time she has moved abruptly and unexpectedly. She has been migrating from one continent to the next, one city to the next, one house to the next all her life. Every three or four years, without fail, out come the boxes, and in go the possessions. Nothing is left behind.

The new houses, however, no matter how lavish, how spacious, how sunny or dark, always seem to require major renovations. It begins with a wall removed here, a door placed there, a window enlarged, a patio enclosed, a bathroom added, a bedroom turned into two, a closet remade into a wall desk unit, an elevator installed, a fireplace inserted, the roof raised, and on and on it goes, for the full three to four years. When the house has nothing more that can be modified without repetition, my mother sells it and moves.

I wonder what is fuelling this particular displacement and rack my brain for things I may have done or not done to make her leave, guilt settling over me like a stifling snow.

Most people her age are downsizing, choosing one-storey condos or two-bedroom bungalows that force a reassessment of inventory, the outside world shrinking as friends die or move into long-term facilities. They sell the largest furniture, keep heirlooms and sentimental mementos, and give or throw away the rest. Not my mother. Each house is larger than the last, as though she anticipates shopping sprees and home deliveries, as though she intends to hold glamorous parties for dozens of people she has yet to meet; as though she were imagining herself in a different life, and so creates a new space to hold the new her.

When I arrive, she is waiting outside, a carry-on bag beside her, as if she'll leave with whomever arrives first: me or the taxi I hope she's cancelled. She is still beautiful, with high cheekbones, large black eyes she accentuates with bluish eye-shadow, full lips a vibrant red, and hair softly curled around her face. She is petite and always impeccably dressed, like a model about to step onto a catwalk, shoulders back, head held high. Today, she wears a cream linen summer dress and matching silk sweater, and on her feet, strappy sandals. On the drive to the airport, she tells me she has scouted out houses on the Internet and already has appointments to see them. I marvel at her concealment—obviously this plan has been in the works for a while. My brother lives in Ottawa, however, so this is not a totally impulsive selection.

"When are you coming back?" I ask, while we're waiting for an attendant to drive her to the gate.

She shrugs. "I'll call you when I know." Bright and breezy, she quickly embraces me when her ride arrives, gets on the golf cart, and off they go.

I walk back to the car, tears springing to my eyes. She hasn't even asked how I might feel about this move away.

Three days later, she returns because the house she wanted—next door to my brother's house—is already sold. However, the excitement of a new venture has rejuvenated her. She phones a real estate agent and begins packing immediately. Within two weeks, she flies back to Ottawa and buys a house. Then the race is on to sell and move.

In the summer of 2007, much to my bewilderment, she deserted a house she had built from the ground up, a house with seven bedrooms and eight bathrooms, a cathedral foyer and a mammoth granite and maple kitchen, claiming to detest the entire enterprise. She bought a large two-storey rectangular, flat-roofed box, and commenced the metamorphosis, so that by the time she announces this latest move to Ottawa, the box has been transformed into a peaked-roof house with graceful bay windows, a stately porch, an upper patio, skylights, fireplaces and, to accommodate an elevator, the house's depth extended by two metres. ("She blew out the back wall," a neighbour said, both in awe and fear, and I thought about heads exploding, or a terrorist attack, both of which exemplified the state of the house and its occupants under deconstruction.)

Colours of a Woman 1 *(mixed media on paper) by Marven Donati (Verbena)*

The real estate agent, a tall, middle-aged blonde, has asked us to empty the house of most of its furniture, displays, and paintings — something my mother balks at. She is a visual artist and can't imagine bare walls.

"Art must elicit powerful emotions," she says. "A house without art is a desert."

The real estate agent tells her that most people do not want powerful emotions exhibited on their walls. They prefer pretty landscapes in colours that match their sofas and carpets. My mother's paintings are anything but pretty landscapes. They are furious expressions of rage and grief — many from a series she painted after breast cancer, after she was left a widow in her forties, with a young child — my brother — to raise alone. The large paintings stretch across her walls, a mixed-media series of faceless women pieced together, ripped, painted on. I am trying to understand these renovations of the self, through these paintings where she is most exposed. Behind glass, in large scale, the collages of tissue-paper patterns and paint are self-portraits in which she is always naked, subjected to the cold hard stare of viewers, her breasts and thighs pale against a cacophony of colour, against the pattern pieces of a life unstitched, the pencilled broken lines tracing the heart, the tissue cut along the curvature of spine, a seam allowance into the fabric of herself, edges raw to the naked eye. We take the paintings down one by one and bubble-wrap them carefully, to keep them from harm.

DIS-LOCATION

"Let's pack the fragile items first," she says, when I arrive with a carful of boxes. She leads the way to the living room, to her display of pottery, brought from Italy when she came to Canada in 1960. The terracotta vessels vary in size and shape: Gnathian wares, amphorae, a Messapian crater, jars, bowls, various oenochoe, as well as rude ceramics, one of which is my favourite—a small toy pig. The pottery originates in the Apuglia region of Italy, where all my mother's childhood homes are spread. Does she look back through these to her fragmented past? We wrap the pottery carefully in tissue before we place them in the FRAGILE boxes.

Inside her paintings she is always broken, limbs askew, face turned to mirrors, to the reflections of her younger self, astonished that the traces of her albescent life have forged these pale concentric circles, this silence, the colours wan imitations of her hurried loves and lovers.

As we continue to pack, our stress levels rise. Over the years and the incessant moves, I have encouraged her to rid herself of odd furniture and useless objects.

"If you're going to lecture me," she says, "go home. These are my souvenirs."

I know what she really means is *mementos*, the residue of things she preserves, without the things themselves. Once in a move, I found the shards of a broken red crystal goblet she had carried house to house for twenty years, because my father had bought it.

Colours of a Woman 6 *(mixed media on paper) by Marven Donati (Verbena)*

155

TRACKS

We progress to her studio, and begin to bubble-wrap the large canvasses that line one side of the room.

In her paintings she is always a shadow, a doppelgänger men stare at. She is the perfect mirror, the shortcut to themselves. What they don't see is that her naked flesh is thick and clothed in quills and scales, a carapace of her own design. Once she used words and touch like broken glass. A tenuous highway, fields of naked limbs against red lips and blood-orange skies.

I am trying to understand her better. I am trying to see her as she is in the paintings, pale, frail, a cut-and-paste, the extra in a movie, always going up stairways.

I return to the house, day after day, help her fill boxes with objects I've seen in so many houses, so many reincarnations. I am silent and anxious, yet aware of her exhaustion.

"Why don't you go lie down for a while?" I say. "I can carry on."

"You think there's time to lie down?" she says, as if I've suggested she take a cruise.

"I don't need you to micromanage me packing," I say.

"These are my things," she says.

"Half of this stuff is junk," I say, and sigh loudly, then wander off to another room. She must be anxious too, but my mother and I conceal our emotions from each other; we speak in gestures and subtext. I am relieved when my brother arrives from Ottawa to help.

During each of these moves, I write furiously in my journal, peppering my comments with rhetorical questions, sparing no excessive punctuations marks — *Why can't she be still???! Why can't she relax for a moment???!! Why can't she just live!!!???* — filling the pages with resentment and rage at the constant upheaval of our lives, to which she seems completely oblivious. If I read back my journals at three- or four-year intervals, the same words confront me, the same emotions, and I am astounded by the constancy of her restlessness and my outrage.

I am no stranger to restlessness, having displaced myself every three or four years, as if I have inherited her need for change. In the past decade, I have settled into one house, though I continue to travel as a means of escape. Like my mother, I have lived on two continents, various provinces and cities, and in three different languages. Yet, despite my love of movement, I am exhausted by my mother's constant relocation, as if she were forever trying to distract or escape herself.

As we continue to load the expanse of her possessions into pods, familiar items emerge, reform themselves into a pattern. The fragments carried house to house derive from each of those abodes she inhabits, constructs and deconstructs, then abandons. (What does she keep of me? I wonder.) She is the archeologist, mining her own creations.

My brother and I carry out a fauteuil my father stripped and stained and reupholstered, from the Kitimat, BC period (1960-1966) when my mother left Italy and joined my father in Canada after his first heart attack at thirty-three. In those six years, they lived in three different houses.

From the West Vancouver house (1967-1969), she carried breast cancer — evident in the paintings — the women's bodies slashed across the chest, the words *cut here* ↓ above a tissue-pattern line. My father collected her and took her to New Brunswick. They were happy there for two short years.

"Are you taking those?" I say to my mother, pointing to the two red leather stick-back chairs from the Bathurst, N.B. house (1970-1972). She and my father leaned their easels on these, so that the leather is stippled with multicoloured paint, like a heart muscle blocked and veined.

She frowns, as if I've suggested she throw away diamonds. "You don't understand," she says, shaking her head.

But I do understand that these objects are replacements for loss. Place-keepers. Markers. The real losses stay within.

In the garage, I find a piece of the Vancouver Cartier house (1973-1984) she lived in after my father died. She removed the carved oak mantelpiece, as if to bring the heart/h to each new house, where it has assumed various guises: faux fireplace, TV stand, the outer edges of an étagère, metamorphosing as needed, as she does. She spent the longest time in this house, and remarried twice instead, a different form of renovation.

"Come help me with this," my brother says, carefully rolling out the black-and-white mosaic tabletop my mother salvaged from the White Rock years (1984-1990). She constructed it from Italian tiles she and her new husband brought back from Italy, each piece broken and reshaped to fit the circle, her life a compulsive repetition, a Goldilocks complex.

Some summers (1984-92), my mother was a tortoise, her house around her, travelling with my stepfather in a panel van she refitted with kitchen, bedroom, bathroom, shower and running water. They drove to the redwoods of California, braved the heat of Death Valley, picked pine nuts in the micro-climates of Arizona, hiked in the red stone canyons of Utah, read under cottonwoods, dreamt under star-filled skies; my mother sketched the landscapes, captured the wild, unyielding desert lands, the buttes and hoodoos like gravestones across red earth. When they sold the van, she kept a bolt of grey upholstery fabric, an unravelling.

The Pine Street house she lived in twice, in 1990-94 and again in 1998-2002. What remains is the tête-à-tête table custom-made to match the kitchen countertop, as if to preserve the intimacy of two people seated by the back door, hibiscus and oleanders in pots beside them.

In between the Pine Street stints, she gutted and renovated her 12th Avenue house (1994-98), and when she left, she unscrewed the built-in wall spice rack (oh, the symbolism here, the scents and pungent disappointments) and uses it in her art studio to hold small jars of paint.

Before this present house was the King Edward house (2002-2007), the one she designed and built, yet from which she unearthed only plants, as if she wanted nothing permanent to remind her. The perfect house turned out to be the one she hated most.

Another house spent. The moving truck winces with the remnants of three continents bulged in boxes. My mother carries all her burdens from place to place. Already her eyes are filled with other skies, her feet tapping, divining, always sure this time, this place, this house...her feet/my feet wanting to map new soils.

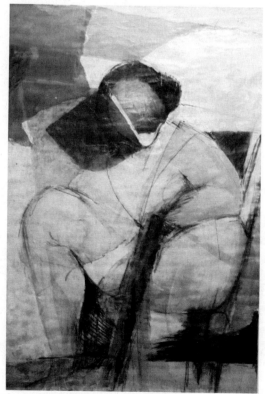

Pattern Shift *(mixed media on paper) by Marven Donati (Verbena)*

REFERENCES

Jon Krakauer, *Into the Wild*, (New York: Anchor Books, Doubleday, 1997).

John Gambetta, Ed., *"Can We Trust Trust?" Trust: Making and Breaking*, (New Jersey: Basil Blackhead Limited, 1988).

John Murray, *A Handbook for Travellers in India, Burma and Ceylon* , (Calcutta: THACKER, SPINK, k 00, 1901), Burma.

Frank J. Spera, *Encyclopedia of Volcanoes*, (Academic Press, 2001).

Iyer, Pico. "Why We Travel." *SALON*, March 18, 2000. http://www.salon.com/2000/03/18/why/ (accessed August 29, 2013).

George J. Firmage, Ed. *The Complete Poems: 1904 - 1962 by E. E. Cummings*, (Liveright Publishing Corporation, 1992).

Henry Miller, *The Henry Miller Reader*, (NY: New Directions Publishing Corporation, 1969).

Henri Michaux, *Stroke by Stroke*, (NY: Archipelago Books, 2006).

Toni Morrison, *"The Site of Memory." What Moves at the Margin: Selected Nonfiction*, (Jackson, MS: University Press of Mississippi, 2008).

Maya Angelou, *I Know Why the Caged Bird Sings*, (NY: Ballantine Books, 2009).

ECO-AUDIT
Printing this book using Rolland Enviro 100 Book
instead of virgin fibres paper saved the following resources:

Trees	Solid Waste	Water	Air Emissions
2	130kg	8,612 L	339 kg